HOW WRITING FACULTY WRITE

HOW WRITING FACULTY WRITE

Strategies for Process, Product, and Productivity

CHRISTINE E. TULLEY

UTAH STATE UNIVERSITY PRESS
Logan

Published by Utah State University Press
An imprint of University Press of Colorado
245 Century Circle, Suite 202
Louisville, CO 80027

Manufactured in the United States of America

ASSOCIATION of UNIVERSITY PRESSES
The University Press of Colorado is a proud member of the Association of University Presses.

The University Press of Colorado is a cooperative publishing enterprise supported, in part, by Adams State University, Colorado State University, Fort Lewis College, Metropolitan State University of Denver, Regis University, University of Colorado, University of Northern Colorado, Utah State University, and Western State Colorado University.

∞ This paper meets the requirements of the ANSI/NISO Z39.48-1992 (Permanence of Paper)

ISBN: 978-1-60732-661-8 (paperback)
ISBN: 978-1-60732-662-5 (ebook)
DOI: https://doi.org/10.7330/9781607326625

Library of Congress Cataloging-in-Publication Data

Names: Tulley, Christine, author.
Title: How writing faculty write : strategies for process, product, and productivity / Christine E. Tulley.
Description: Logan : Utah State University Press, [2018] | Includes bibliographical references and index.
Identifiers: LCCN 2017025379| ISBN 9781607326618 (pbk.) | ISBN 9781607326625 (ebook)
Subjects: LCSH: Academic writing. | Manuscript preparation (Authorship) | College teachers—Interviews. | College teachers as authors.
Classification: LCC P301.5.A27 T85 2018 | DDC 808.02—dc23

LC record available at https://lccn.loc.gov/2017025379

To Ted Lardner, who introduced me to the field of rhetoric and composition, and to Kristine Blair, who served as my first role model for a productive career as a scholarly writer. Special thanks to my husband, Ron, and my daughters, Devon and Deana, who gave me the support and time I needed to complete the project.

CONTENTS

PREFACE

In 1953, the *Paris Review* began publishing a series of interviews with writers of the day, including Truman Capote, Dorothy Parker, and William Faulkner. During *Review* editor visits to their homes and writing studios, interviewees were asked how specific works came to fruition as well as general questions about the writing process. The purpose of the "Writers at Work" interview series was to offer a chance for writers to talk about the backstory of published works where "the interviews read like good conversation" unlike traditional literary criticism (Brooks 1963, 6). The interviews provided a fascinating snapshot of how authors find ideas, struggle with writer's block, approach revision, and navigate publication venues—certainly relevant issues to teachers of writing but also to faculty struggling with publication.

As a professor of rhetoric and composition and part-time faculty developer who coaches faculty writers, I've long been fascinated by the messiness of moving writing from idea to final publication *Review* interviews bring to light. Every choice from idea generation, to phrasing, to revision strategies, to the time of day to work on writing from each writer provides a collective picture of productive writing habits for the most successful writers over the past sixty years.

From working with faculty writing groups and tenure and promotion workshops, I am acutely aware of the struggles faculty of all disciplines face with writing, particularly in attitudes toward writing where frustration, fear, and shame are common and in areas where they lack strategies for process (starting and restarting a writing project), product (moving a project to completion), and productivity (developing habits to ensure process and product thrive). *How Writing Faculty Write* replicates The *Paris Review* interview process by providing the back story about the academic writing habits of "rock star" rhetoric and composition faculty to learn what makes them successful. Perhaps more importantly, the interviewees also capture how writing faculty differ from other faculty writers, and therefore the interviews also offer a novel way to think about faculty writing practices as an area of research for the discipline. As Jonathan Alexander (2015, 383) argues in his first editorial piece as *College Composition and Communication* editor: "The production of questions about writing is what our discipline is all about." In addition to providing specific answers about how writing faculty write, it is my hope that the collection prompts new questions about faculty writing practices within rhetoric and composition.

ACKNOWLEDGMENTS

How Writing Faculty Write reveals writing faculty never write alone, and this project is no different. First, a sincere thanks to the interviewees who selflessly and generously offered open and revealing descriptions of their writing processes. I'd also like to thank the inaugural class of Master of Arts in Rhetoric and Writing students at The University of Findlay who transcribed interviews so meticulously: Pam Cochran, Jamie Erford, Robert Ryder, Lauren Salisbury, Derek Sherman, and Ginny Stoller. I can't think of a better introduction to the field or start to our new MA degree in Rhetoric and Writing. A special thanks to Kathi Yancey who suggested Utah State University Press as the best match for this project and to editors Michael Spooner, Laura Furney, and reviewers who helped shape the project into a resource for the field. Though the project looks different from what I had first imagined, I'm thrilled with the results. Two other colleagues who made this project better are Emily Walling, who helped me with structural touches, and Lauren Salisbury, who helped me with insightful feedback from the point of view of a future faculty member. And finally a very heartfelt thanks to Louise Wetherbee Phelps, friend and colleague, who helped me think through structural arguments for this book. Louise gave me the final push to help me articulate some of the more complex arguments in *How Writing Faculty Write.*

HOW WRITING FACULTY WRITE

INTRODUCTION

Faculty Writing as a Research Area for Rhetoric and Composition

Much of our scholarship within the field of rhetoric and composition focuses on how writing "happens." We've studied the composing processes of twelfth graders, first-year composition classes, adult learners, workplace writers, community college students, non-native speakers, and the incarcerated, among other populations. We've even studied faculty writers from other disciplines (for two examples, see Eodice and Geller 2013 and Thaiss and Zawacki 2006). But the writing processes rhetoric and composition faculty use to compose the intellectual labor and scholarship of our field—the oft-cited monographs, the award-winning articles, the textbooks, the edited collections, and the new media essays that include films, images, sounds, and hyperlinks—are largely a mystery. In short, we know very little about how *writing* faculty write.

This lack of self-study of our own writing habits is disconcerting for several reasons. For one, writing is our field of study. The field of rhetoric and composition investigates the most effective composing strategies under a variety of conditions and within a range of contexts. From the research we conduct and the textbooks we publish, writing faculty, we might assume, "know" the tricks of effective writing and how to navigate issues that faculty of all disciplines often struggle with: combatting writer's block, juggling multiple deadlines, representing research accurately and fairly, etc. We might even assume that writing faculty have more tools for academic writing success than faculty in other disciplines. Because rhetoric and composition faculty share the writing challenges of the interviewees featured here: no time to write, heavy teaching loads, etc., learning the strategies successful faculty writers use within a variety of contexts is key for understanding how to ground and potentially improve faculty writing practices within the discipline. Yet beyond preliminary research by Wells (2015) and Soderlund (2015) and a few essays on how collaborative academic writing between writing faculty affects careers in the field (see Day and Eodice 2001; Ede and Lunsford 2001; Ronald and Roskelly 2001; Yancey and Spooner 1998), we've only

DOI: 10.7330/9781607326625.c000

been working around the edges of a conversation about our composing practices as faculty. We ultimately don't know if field-based knowledge shapes our own academic writing practices or influences our scholarly output as authors of rhetoric and composition publications, yet faculty writing within rhetoric and composition is a rich area of study central to our broader mission of studying how writing works.

Moreover, writing faculty have a discipline-driven, philosophical impetus to write. Unlike other academic disciplines, a key tenet in the field of rhetoric and writing is that writing teachers *should be writers.* A disciplinary identity as a writer differs from the way that other academics define themselves, as faculty in other disciplines choose instead to think of themselves as "readers or problem solvers or project managers or scientists" (Geller 2013, 7; Toor 2015). In contrast we are *writing* faculty in both senses of the term. Rhetoric and composition scholars such as Richard Gebhardt (1977), Maxine Hairston (1986), Donald Murray (1986), and E. Shelley Reid (2009) argue that writing teachers, especially, have an obligation to write because the process of writing and the teaching of writing are inseparable. As rationale, Hairston argues,

> Teachers who do not engage in the writing process themselves cannot adequately understand the complex dynamics of the process, cannot empathize with their students' problems, and are in no position either to challenge or to endorse the recommendations and admonitions of the textbooks they are using. (Hairston 1986, 62)

This goal is so essential; it has remained the number one expectation for training writing teachers since the Conference on College Composition and Communication (1982) issued a position statement on the preparation of writing teachers in 1982. And many faculty *do* write both with students in classes and in reflective activity outside of class (see Eng 2002 for a useful overview). In National Writing Project workshops and similar professional development activities such as the Institute for Writing and Thinking at Bard College, instructors primarily write as part of learning to teach writing more effectively. Gebhardt (1977, 140) makes the case for these efforts, arguing writing teachers should write about the teaching of writing as a mode of learning, as a means of both understanding and arguing for personal practices and theories. Likewise, Brannon and Pradl (1994) consider the dual identities of writing teacher and writer as inseparable. Still, despite repeated research suggesting that engaging in writing is essential to be an effective writing teacher, the field of rhetoric and composition has not explored how our disciplinary connection influences the writing that is the academic currency of most tenure-track and tenured positions.

Equally important, we should not overlook the fact that many of us *like* to write and chose to become writing teachers as a result. In contrast, our counterparts in other disciplines often dislike academic writing and struggle to compose (Boice 1990; Dwyer et al. 2012; Fairweather 1999), requiring interventions from department chairs and faculty developers to motivate them (Eodice and Cramer 2001; Geller and Denny 2013; Lechuga and Lechuga 2012). Faculty who teach writing understand that writing for a specific audience and having published work recognized among peers is both motivating and rewarding, because the process of writing itself is intellectually satisfying and engaging. As Donald Murray (1986) points out, "publishing promises a lifetime of exploration and learning, active membership in a scholarly community, and the opportunity for composition teachers to practice what we preach" (146). While we also compose for non-peer reviewed venues such as scholarly blogs, articles for *The Chronicle of Higher Education* or *Inside Higher Education,* lecture videos and podcasts, as a field we still appreciate well written peer reviewed scholarship and rely on such work for our own research and to make cases about our writing centers and programs. Rhetoric and composition scholars understand the inherent value in academic writing, but the writing habits that lead to publications and make some writing faculty highly productive in terms of scholarly output are, for the most part, invisible.

Learning more about our own faculty writing practices also might serve our political interests as a discipline. Rhetoric and composition has historically struggled to overcome the reputation as a service discipline for a legitimate place within higher education. Faculty publication is an investment most universities are interested in because publications and grants offer academic recognition, donor opportunities, and funding avenues. The university stands much to gain the more published and prolific its faculty members are. A faculty that knows how to write is a more attractive payoff to administrators than getting the majority of student writers through first year writing (especially when there is a financial incentive to have students repeat classes). It's also expensive when faculty members are denied tenure because they don't write. Given the increased emphasis within higher education on faculty performance and accountability (Bellas and Toutkoushian 1999; Fairweather 2002; Hardré and Kollmann 2012; Lincoln 2011; Savage 2003), study of academic publishing patterns (Baldwin and Chandler 2002; Henderson 2011), and faculty motivations for publishing (Hardré et al. 2011; Tien and Blackburn 1996), and the concern for the well-being of the professoriate (Stupnisky, Weaver-Hightower, and Kartoshkina 2015), rhetoric and writing faculty can play a key role in understanding the relationship between faculty members' writing habits and job success. Writing faculty can offer an educated knowledge base about the academic writing process vs. general faculty development efforts which tend to focus on productivity and don't always work (Brown 2014; Webber 2011).

Finally, and most important, in our field there are graduate students, faculty members at all ranks, untenured Writing Program Administrators (WPAs)/Writing Center Professionals (WCPs), and adjuncts struggling to write. In a 1985 *College Composition and Communication* article, Robert Boice suggests composition as a field tends to focus on process and product within the classroom, but neglects productivity—the regular output of publishable material in unstructured spaces beyond the classroom—and this carries over to publishing habits of writing faculty. He argues,

> the prescriptions of composition researchers seem to apply only to the context in which they typically do their research and theorizing—the classroom within an academic semester or, more often, within a few sessions of writing. In my experience, the same people who had excelled in writing classes may not have learned to write in other settings—where guidelines are ambiguous, where writing is easily put off, and where the consequences of writing include promotion and tenure. (Boice 1985, 473)

Despite knowing academic writing as a discipline, many of us aren't doing it. Maxine Hairston's research affirms what Boice describes, commenting "almost any publishing academic with whom I have talked about their writing admits having trouble" (Hairston 1986, 64). While two specifically rhetoric and composition-focused writing advice guides exist (Olson and Taylor's 1997 *Publishing in Rhetoric and Composition* and Gebhardt and Gebhardt's 1997 *Academic Advancement in Composition Studies*), both are two decades old and the conversation has not progressed much since. In contrast to the dated nature of rhetoric and composition resources for faculty writing assistance, fields such as nursing actively work as a field to prepare graduate students and colleagues for academic writing, and publish several new articles a year on how to write (Steinert et al. 2008). While our discipline is not alone in neglecting graduate writing (see Brooks-Gillies et al. 2015; Caplan and Cox 2016; Grego and Thompson 2007; Rose and McClafferty 2001; Russell 2002; Sallee, Hallett, and Tierney 2011), increasing calls for more explicit graduate writing instruction within the field of rhetoric and composition continue to emerge (Micciche and Carr 2011; Soderlund 2015; Wells 2015). And though field specific time management issues have been studied (Boice 1985; Enos 1990, 1996), research is needed as to how WPAs/WCPs and faculty who teach composition actually manage to write despite these time constraints. Due to a lack of knowledge about optimal field-based writing practices, most new rhetoric and writing faculty learn what little they know about academic writing within writing studies on the job (Soderlund 2015; Wells 2015). For all of these reasons noted above, the time is opportune for rhetoric and composition to study disciplinary faculty writing practices for publication.

What we *do* know about faculty productivity in rhetoric and composition is that the nature of our discipline puts us in danger of not completing the writing so essential in most academic positions for tenure and job security. With scholarly "productivity" typically defined as the number of publications at most institutions (Fairweather 1999; Gebhardt and Gebhardt 1997; Olson and Taylor 1997; Tien and Blackburn 1996; Townsend and Rosser, 2007), having time to devote to academic writing for publication is essential. And time is one resource rhetoric and composition faculty often don't have. Our faculty positions are simultaneously tied to time intensive marking of papers and to time intensive administration as WPAs, WCPs, or writing across the curriculum (WAC) coordinators. We spend more time grading and conferencing than our counterparts in other fields (Applebee 1977; Connors 1990; Naylor and Malcomson 2001) because, unlike other disciplines such as literature or history, composition requires an "individualized pedagogy" (Connors 1990, 110). Practically translated, this means that a writing instructor must individually comment or conference on each student paper at least some of the time. Assuming that an instructor of introductory composition might assign three or four papers per semester, plus rough drafts, the workload is demanding. Interest in multimodal composition has also increased the time needed to prepare for teaching, as instructors must attend to student technology concerns and learn how to teach using technology resources—further straining a heavy workload (Bernhardt, Edwards, and Wojahn 1989; Dangler 2010; Reinheimer 2005; Takayoshi and Selfe 2007; Tulley 2008). In one study, faculty who spent more time on teaching produced up to 10 percent fewer publications or similar research projects (Webber 2011; see other scholarship by Fox 1992; Townsend and Rosser 2007; Trice 1992), and teaching effectively in writing studies takes more time than in other disciplines. Narratives within the field offer cautionary tales about how teaching and service affect progress toward tenure (see Danberg 2011; Gindlesparger 2011; Leverenz 2000). Writing faculty, in other words, are at higher risk of not writing for publication because they have to allocate more time to teaching.

Moreover, because many faculty positions in rhetoric and composition come with an administrative assignment to direct a WAC initiative, first-year composition program, or writing center, our discipline is especially susceptible to the paradoxical impulse to be a good university citizen versus productive faculty member. Writing program or center administrators have a difficult and daily choice to make as to how to allocate time—do they "focus on the success of the center or program which is what the institution values or publishing which matters for career advancement and dissemination of our field knowledge?" (Geller and Denny 2013, 103). Administrative positions often expand to include all writing-related issues on campus, including encompassing abstract issues such as "Our students can't write; what are you going to do about it?" (Smith 2008, 123). Consequently, rhetoric and composition faculty serve time on consuming administrative and accreditation related projects even during summers and breaks instead of using this time for academic writing. Due to these field-specific productivity challenges, explicit knowledge of what it means to be a rhetoric and composition faculty member who writes is sorely needed. We know what circumstances hinder some rhetoric and composition faculty from writing for scholarly publication, but little about the disciplinary practices that make successful writing faculty productive.

As a response to this gap, this study takes as its focus the project of finding out how writing faculty write. Using the *Paris Review* "Writers at Work" model, I asked fifteen rhetoric and composition faculty with significant publications or growing influence in the field about their writing processes, as well as how teaching, administration, and service influence publication rates. Through a series of interviews with these productive, prolific scholars in our field, I investigated question such as:

- What do the writing habits of writing faculty look like?
- Do we follow disciplinary advice about best writing practices?
- How do we convey our experiential knowledge about writing to our students?
- How do we collaboratively write for academic publication?
- How does our work as editors in the field affect our own writing?
- How do we balance writing with notoriously heavy service, administration, and teaching loads?
- What does it mean to be a writing professor who writes within the disciplinary location of rhetoric and composition?

In his introduction to the first series of *Review* interviews, editor Malcom Cowley remarks that despite the diversity of interviewees, "what emerges from the interviews is a composite picture of the fiction writer" (Cowley 1967, 6). The goal of *How Writing Faculty Write* is to provide a similar composite picture of rhetoric and composition faculty within the following chapters. The interviews about writing processes not only reveal answers to the above questions but, as a collective, provide a snapshot of how we view our own writing as a field. Maintaining the conversational spirit of the *Paris Review*–style interviews, the goal is not to present the "right" way to compose or a definitive picture of the writing habits of rhetoric and composition faculty. Instead, the collection offers a more nuanced and varied scope of how writing scholarship is produced. In their own words, faculty describe their writing habits, time management strategies, how they feel when they write, how they cope with writer's block, and more, including the backstories behind many landmark works in the field. For faculty productivity research within writing studies, the interviews, taken together, offer strategies for both graduate students and writing faculty for maintaining a writing schedule, getting started and restarted, juggling multiple writing projects, and serving their disciplines *and* their institutions successfully.

As noted in the Preface, I was initially inspired by the *Paris Review* interviews because these dialogues capture writers talking about how they write. Encouraging writing faculty to talk more openly and explicitly about their writing processes offers rich terrain for what it means to be a professor who writes. In the following sections I argue for the *Review* interview style as a deliberate methodology and ideally suited for this type of research. I follow with a brief introduction to the interviewees and several patterns for analysis that emerge from the interviews. These patterns illustrate, as a group, interviewees share two attitudes of accepting the academic writing process as messy and challenging and finding joy in building a work for publications. They also share three recurrent writing techniques of thinking rhetorically, using invention strategies that scaffold writing, and calling on "quick focus" to write in the short time segments they have available. I conclude with a readers' guide to help specific populations (graduate students, mid-career administrators, established faculty, and writing researchers) use *How Writing Faculty Write* as a resource.

THE *PARIS REVIEW*–STYLE INTERVIEW AS A METHODOLOGY

For this project the *Paris Review*–style interview was aptly matched to the types of interviews about writing processes I wanted to conduct. Like the *Review* interviews of famous literary writers whose work was featured in the magazine, I wanted to interview well-known writers within the discipline. The *Review* interviews worked well largely due to the fact that interviewees were asked unstructured questions about writing and the conversation could take a natural direction. Though unstructured interviews do have drawbacks such as a lack of reliability because each interview is unique, when an *aide memoire* or agenda is used to establish similar topics that might be covered in each interview (i.e., questions about how to start writing, best time of day to write, etc.), there is "a certain degree of consistency across different interview sessions" (Zhang and Wildemuth 2009) useful for general analysis (Briggs 2000; Minichiello et al. 1990).

To model the *Review* interviews as closely as possible, I developed open ended questions similar to those established by Cowley and maintained the *Review*'s practice of tailoring questions to each writer. Though interviewees were asked similar questions about how they start a writing project, avoid writer's block, revise, etc., other questions were personalized to the interviewee (e.g., Joe Harris revised one of his most well-known works, and a question of how he revised himself was asked). Therefore, the interview questions were unstructured in nature, but not all participants received the same unstructured interview questions (see appendix for a list of typical *Review*-style questions used in the interviews featured in this collection).

I also followed *Review* interview protocols as closely as possible with technological updates. Early interviews of literary authors were done by two reviewers, as Cowley describes:

> Interviewers usually worked in pairs, like FBI agents. Since no recording equipment was available for the early interviews, they both jotted down the answers to their questions at top speed and matched the two versions afterward. With two men writing, the pace could be kept almost at the level of natural conversation. Some of the later interviews . . . were done with a tape recorder. After two or three sessions the interviewers typed up their material; then it was cut to length, arranged in logical order, and sent to the author for his approval. (Cowley 1967, 5)

I updated the recording aspect by using Skype to record digital interviews and a digital audio recorder to record face to face interviews. However, to mimic the early partner protocol described above, two graduate students transcribed the recorded interviews and I compared versions for a match due to potential variations in emphasis during transcription. Though interviews were also cut to length, most were preserved in the order the questions were asked. Interviewees were also sent copies of their interviews for clarification and approval.

Rather than coding the interviews for analysis down to keywords and specific themes in a manner similar to thematic network analysis (see Attride-Stirling 2001), the original *Review* interviews were read for broad patterns by editor Malcom Cowley ("Let's see how they go about their daily task of inventing stories and putting them on paper") (Cowley 1967, 7). I chose to read interviews in a similar manner. While coding is valuable, and can provide a level of detail not featured in this collection, participants were not asked the same open-ended questions central for coding effectively (Scott and Garner 2013). Like the original analysis of *Review* interviews by Cowley (1967), I used answers to similar interview questions (e.g., "How do you get started on a writing project?" or a variation) to determine what general habits the majority of writers follow. These patterns for analysis are presented in the following section.

Mode of publication is also a methodological choice, and I do recognize that our discipline, perhaps more so than others, has sought to argue for a wider understanding of scholarship. A printed book highlighting traditional faculty publication practices might seem to undermine this project. Rhetoric and composition has struggled as a field with how to reconcile digital scholarship, including issues of open access, with the traditional peer-reviewed print expectations of the institutions where we work (Ball 2004; Look and Pinter 2010). There is no doubt that "our work in rhetoric and composition suffers under the definition of what constitutes scholarship" (Enos 1996, 13) as activities central to our discipline such as writing program administration (including WAC efforts), writing center administration, software development, textbook publication, and journal editing are neither recognized as scholarly nor given equal weight as traditional publication in tenure and promotion processes (Alred and Thelen 1993; Enos 1996; Thaiss and Zawacki 2006).

As a former WPA, I certainly support a wider definition of scholarship after having firsthand experience with the effort required to publish the required number of items in case my administrative work did not count for tenure. I wholeheartedly agree more progress is needed in this area. Yet, our discipline, like others in the humanities, "[persists] in an academic culture rooted in dissemination and vetting of original work, intellectual capital on the page that confers and accrues in powerful ways" and as a result, "The quantity and quality of published scholarship is crucial to one's ethos as a 'real' academic" (Geller and Denny 2013, 118). To succeed on the tenure track our intellectual labor typically must include knowledge dissemination through traditional outlets in addition to making arguments for dissemination and evaluation through other venues (e.g., through a Council of Writing Program

Administrators' review of a writing program to determine the value of a WPA's scholarship).

With this recognition in mind, I deliberately focus many of the interview questions on the production and publication of monographs, textbooks, edited collections, and peer-reviewed articles in both print and digital formats. Some of these "count" more than others for tenure and promotion depending on local context, but all reflect the labor of getting words on the page or screen. This labor directly translates to success as a writing professor in the current academic environment. As Peter Elbow and Mary Deane Sorcinelli neatly sum up: "Professors write things. If they don't write things, they don't get to be professors (Elbow and Sorcinelli 2006, 19). Despite the push to expand scholarship to include other types of work, productive, regular writing, and publication of peer-reviewed scholarship from that writing, remains key to most successful careers as rhetoric and composition professors. The *Paris Review* methodology is well suited to find out how professors write for academic publication.

More important, from a methodological perspective, part of the appeal of the original *Review* interviews was that when read together, they offered a narrative about how writing happens within a community of writers. I argue a similar narrative manifests in *How Writing Faculty Write*—readers of these interviews can likewise see who "writers are as persons, where they get their material, how they work from day to day, and what they dream of writing" (Cowley 1967, 4).

ABOUT THE INTERVIEWEES

After informally asking graduate students and faculty across all ranks whose writing practices they wanted to know more about at conferences and via email, I sent out twenty initial email invitations based on the most frequently mentioned names. Fifteen accepted an interview invitation. Not surprisingly, many in the field wanted to know about the habits of past and present journal editors and disciplinary organization presidents who published regularly—some of the busiest people in the discipline—because they wanted to know how these prolific colleagues managed to write. As a result, seven interviewees are former Conference on College Composition and Communication (CCCC) chairs (Anson, Harris Glenn, Powell, Royster, Selfe, Tinberg, and Yancey) and past presidents of the Council of Writing Program Administrators (Anson, Roen, and Yancey). There are also seven past and present journal editors featured (Alexander, Blair, Harris, Powell, Selfe, Tinberg, and Yancey). Many interviewees (Blair, Enoch, Roen, Royster, and Yancey) are current or former WPAs, WAC coordinators, writing center directors, or university administrators who are well aware of time conflicts posed by administration. In addition to disciplinary leadership both on their campuses and within the discipline, the interviewees have won the highest awards for scholarship in our field and beyond, some at the earliest stages of their careers (Enoch, Rickert, and Yergeau). Beyond the accomplishments, interviewees have taught 4–4 loads and all served on multiple university committees. This mix of experience combined with publication success makes them ideal candidates for interviews about the academic writing process.

As a caveat, I recognize that the interviewees featured here are not typical of many rhetoric and composition faculty, or faculty in general. Like *Review* interviewees, they are accomplished members of the field and were similarly selected for interviews as a result of their publication achievements. The faculty featured here have either tenure track or tenured positions and are those among the lucky few with privileged positions in a field that has a history of overworked, underpaid labor and untenured administrators. Yet a view of how successful writing faculty write is a useful starting point for broader study of faculty writing practices in rhetoric and composition. Like all published authors, at some point they had to compose using a pen and paper, or a keyboard, microphone, or web or video authoring software. Moreover, most of the faculty featured here have served or are serving in the time intensive positions as writing center directors, writing program administrators, chairs of undergraduate departments and graduate programs, student success center directors, and teaching excellence center directors. They have experienced firsthand the time constraints within rhetoric and composition known to derail writing productivity, yet have developed productive writing strategies despite these conditions. Though most are currently working at Research 1 (R1) institutions, many have previously served as faculty members at small liberal arts colleges, regional state schools, and comprehensive universities where teaching loads and service loads are high and still managed to publish regularly early in their careers. Every interview chapter starts with a headnote to contextualize interviewees' working contexts. Interviewees also hail from many corners of the field: writing program administration, Native American rhetorics, computers and composition, feminist historiography, and more; together they provide a rich and varied picture of the writing practices used to compose the still-developing field rhetoric and composition. In the following section, I provide an overview of patterns for analysis that emerge from reading the interviews as a whole.

HOW *ARE* WRITING FACULTY WRITING? PATTERNS FOR ANALYSIS

Despite variances in writing strategies and local contexts, several patterns emerge from the interviews. These patterns are useful for illustrating what interviewees know about academic writing from their insider location in the discipline and what writing faculty articulate about themselves as writers. Though interviewees also adopt strategies that productive faculty across disciplines use—relying on a multiple project planning system, developing a plan for writing with collaborators before the project gets underway, and combining writing projects with other faculty responsibilities such as teaching or service—contextual knowledge of writing and its influence on the composing process clearly emerges in these conversations. As fellow writing faculty Donald Murray reminds us, "If we can discover the attitudes and the techniques that allow us to write we will experience the joy of writing" (Murray 1986, 153), and the interviewees offer first glimpses of what these attitudes and resulting writing techniques look like within our discipline. The writing techniques of thinking rhetorically, using invention strategies that scaffold, and quick focus to write in short bursts described in the introduction tell us what writing faculty *do* when they write, and the attitudes described below tell us how they *feel* when they write. Both behaviors and attitudes are necessary for successful, and more important, workable academic writing habits in today's writing faculty positions. These broad patterns encompass a combination of process, product, and productivity strategies Boice (1985) notes are essential for rhetoric and composition faculty academic publishing success.

Attitudes that Allow Writing

Writing Faculty Accept the Writing Process as Difficult and Persist through Frustration

Interview research suggests that writing faculty succeed because they tacitly accept a key tenet of our field: academic writing, like all writing, is a recursive, messy, and sometimes frustrating learning process. Perhaps surprisingly, the interviews reveal that disciplinary knowledge does not translate into making the academic writing process easier for writing faculty. Like the *Paris Review* interviewees who initially inspired this collection, faculty featured here are also "writers at work," and the work is sometimes, well, work. Though the stereotype of the English major/English professor as a fluent writer may persist (Reid 2009), interviewees admitted to struggling with academic writing for a variety of reasons despite knowing invention strategies, techniques for revision, grammar rules, and even experiencing previous publication success. Sometimes the challenge is just getting started; a familiar problem for academics across disciplines (Belcher 2009; Carnell et al. 2008; Scott 2014). Howard Tinberg admits in his interview, "Writing has never come easily for me so it can be a bit of struggle to get the meaning out and onto the screen," and Cindy Selfe agrees, noting, "I slog through my scholarly work." Sometimes the difficulty stems from the scope and vastness of a new project, as when Selfe describes her writing process as "a slow, hard slog through materials, collecting the materials, doing the research if I'm doing the research or finding the scholarly sources and then fitting them together in a way that makes sense to me." Malea Powell agrees that managing scope is a problem that takes time to address remarking, "I frequently struggle with how to chop giant ideas down to size." Developing an appropriate methodology to use is another challenge that slows down writing when starting to write for publication as Cheryl Glenn describes: "Nobody had any methodology for me to use, so it took me several years to develop a feminist, historiographic methodology, a lens through which to read my materials and write my work." Faculty also mentioned speed of writing as a factor. Jessica Enoch explains: "I see myself as a slow writer because I feel like I write very slowly. If someone told me to write a ten-page paper by tomorrow, I would not be able to do that. I write very slowly but I write every day . . . I could never write a lot at once." Kris Blair agrees: "I believe in those sorts of adages of 'write a page a day,' 'don't procrastinate,' and others because I'm not a quick writer. I really do need time to think and write badly and then see how the little bad things I've written get better with each passing day."

These writing challenges echo sentiments of faculty outside of rhetoric and composition, as many academic writers experience similar frustrations with getting ideas on paper/screen, clarifying methodology, and even speed of writing. Even from their vast knowledge base of writing practices, rhetoric, and composition, these excerpts illustrate faculty don't necessarily sail through the composing process, confirming previous research by Hairston (1986) and Scott (2014).

As such, there are important lessons to be learned about both frustration and persistence here from the attitude of acceptance of writing difficulty threaded through the interviews. Interviewees understand that sometimes a lot of thinking must happen before words can be captured in print or multimodally, and though spending time on thinking prior to and during writing sessions may be frustrating, it's necessary. Royster describes these bouts of thinking as essential moments of "focusing" prior to writing:

> I've always made the case that the difficult part about writing is not the writing, it's the thinking. You know, getting myself to the point where I feel that I'm thinking well, coherently, and consistently about whatever the topic of concern is the challenge. I want to feel that I'm in focus. I can try to get myself in focus but the real challenge is *feeling* in focus. "Oh yeah, this is where I want to be with this idea. I like this sentence. Oh right, this is a good article that I want to keep in scope or this is the thought that I want to carry from this part to that part." So it's the thinking part. The writing for me has always been a moment of joy.

As Royster's excerpt illustrates, writing faculty often view the thinking moments combined with the writing moments as a larger process of "writing to learn" (Murray 1984). Viewing the writing process as an opportunity for learning, even when difficult, is a different attitude than viewing the academic writing process as merely the capture of research on paper. Even when academics manage to publish regularly, many view writing as a reporting mechanism. This is limiting. As Hayot (2014, 1) argues, "Writing as though you already know what you have to say hinders it as a medium for research and discovery; it blocks the possibilities—the openings—that appear at the intersection of an intention and an audience." The interviews illustrate that writing faculty as a group accept the need to use the early stages of writing to find these openings, and we do follow what we tell first-year writing students: the early stages of writing are for discovering what we want to say as academic writers.

Though writing to learn might be viewed as "procrastinating" from actually writing, watching for the openings Hayot describes is a natural part of this thinking process, a thinking process rhetoric and composition faculty accept as essential. In his interview, Joe Harris reframes procrastination as incubation, and like Royster, claims the need for time to think through projects before and during early process phases. He argues:

> I do think, by the way, that some of that procrastination is actually something more like incubation. When I begin a project, I really have to think about it, and it takes me awhile to sort through what it is that I want to say and to think about how I want to begin and what books I want to have on my desk and so on, and that's not a particularly organized process. It's just a lot of time walking the dogs and walking around the house and thinking about the piece and thinking I should be writing, but yet for some reason not quite being able to do it.

Faculty development literature suggest there is much shame associated with not writing, and shame contributes to blocking, hindering overall productivity (Boice 1990; Hairston 1986; Shahjahan 2014).

Yet excerpts such as the one above illustrate that interviewees don't frame these stops in writing as traditional blocks per se. Here Harris recognizes that incubation does not mean that writing time is wasted; instead incubation *is* the writing process. Chris Anson similarly and cheerfully describes the thinking process as incubation versus a block in writing: "I think I was incubating the CCCC's address for a year [laughs] because I was thinking about it on my runs, and I was thinking, but actually I didn't start it until about three months before." Because interviewees accept struggling to start a writing project as a natural part of the reflective academic writing process, they don't have the sense of panic or shame about non-writing periods that may contribute to blocking (and in fact, only Yergeau ever described being blocked, and then only when dealing with disturbing research she needed to write about).

Moreover, because rhetoric and composition faculty recognize writing is sometimes a struggle, many of the interviewees do have preemptive strategies to keep writing flowing. One common strategy is to switch between writing projects, so writing is never stopped and there is always forward progress on at least one project. Kathi Yancey describes this technique when working on a draft:

> There are sometimes places in the middle where I know something's not working but I don't know what it is and but then what I tend to do is just flip to something else. I've always got something else going on. So I'll go do the something else or I'll take some kind of a break and then I'll come back. I've never had writer's block in the sense that you're spending weeks or months or even days on end unable to write.

Switching projects allows the writer incubation time to work out a problem, but at the same time moves another writing project forward. The interviews demonstrate writing faculty tend to be kinder with themselves about their relationship with academic writing and thus less frustrated with the lifecycle of academic publications. In one *Chronicle of Higher Education* article, Ted McCormick points out that faculty who enjoy the writing process recognize good thinking "can't be forced or even routinized in a reliable way" and take time to reflect (McCormick 2017, n.p.), and the interviewees similarly illustrate an awareness of the importance of reflection to think through writing problems. This attitude may be in part because writing faculty understand from their disciplinary location that "Current composition pedagogy is based on the premise that writing well *is* difficult" (Reid 2009, W202; emphasis mine). Here our disciplinary knowledge is clearly an advantage for academic publication. Rather than leading to paralysis or writer's block, the struggle to write is recast by writing faculty as natural and after an incubation period/writing to learn session they are able to start or restart writing.

Writing Faculty Enjoy Process as Well as Product

Writing faculty interviewed for the collection tend to cast the writing process as a pleasurable activity because they enjoy clarifying and organizing ideas as well as demonstrating writing skill. Kathi Yancey describes what is so satisfying about writing: "It's really within the last five years where I get a lot of pleasure out of revision . . . I like how William Gass talks about 'makingness of a text' and I like the makingness of a text. I like working with words. I like working with document design. I like working with visuals. I like making all of that come together in a composition." DeVoss captures how many writing faculty feel when they first begin a new project: "When I have a chance to write it is the best feeling in the world because I have on my computer probably ten or fifteen different folders with outlines for manuscripts I haven't had a chance to get started on, that at one point I was like, 'Oh my gosh, I have to write this [one manuscript], this is going to be so epic, this is amazing, this needs to be out there! I can pull these students in . . . we'll work on it together and all this is great!'" These responses confirm research from Packer (2013) that when faculty experience satisfaction with the academic writing process it contributes to "gross personal happiness" (85).

Enjoyment with the writing process goes beyond just starting a project. Revision is another area faculty enjoy as it leads to new discoveries, as Thomas Rickert points out: "The most inventive material you will ever come up with comes from working with revising a draft. Typically, my greatest insights will come from that and forcing me to go back and do various forms of revision, but it always comes from working out a problem that I wasn't aware was a problem yet." Joe Harris actually considers the revision of writing, the working toward a finished product as the actual "work" of writing itself and the most pleasurable part of writing: "I really imagine the work of composing at the point of revision rather than the point of invention. That's where I feel more in control. That's where I take more pleasure in craft." This is not to say that revision is necessarily easy—indeed Yancey describes it as an "acquired skill." Yet many interviewees commented specifically on the satisfying, deeper level of engagement writing revision provides and use this satisfaction to work a draft to a finished product.

Experiencing joy from the writing process is another way writing faculty move writing forward. As Jackie Royster argues, "I can get passionate about writing projects and that passion helps me stay in focus. I'm always thinking about the subject even when I'm not working because I'm engaged with the topic." Joy helps writing faculty incubate writing even during non-writing periods, confirming research on the relationship between faculty writing and joy (Packer 2013; Tulley 2013).

Perhaps most important, writing faculty featured here view the overall academic writing process as joyful versus the end publication. Melanie Yergeau notes, "I find putting together a project that matters to me, and hopefully to others, extremely satisfying." Jessica Enoch voices something similar: "[Writing a book has] been really fun. I love it. I mean I love working on it and it's kind of been like a safe thing. I'm working on this book that I really like and I love being able to go to these places and do this archival work, but now I'm pushing towards, I hope, the final quarter and asking 'What am I going to do?' [laughs]." The passion helps use open moments for writing and moving projects forward versus checking email or over-prepping for classes. Writing faculty clearly identify as writers and are productive because they enjoy researching and writing. This behavior confirms previous faculty productivity research by Lechuga and Lechuga who contend "faculty members whose locus of self-worth and identification reside in the domain of scholarly research are more likely to focus their attention to those events that reinforce the value of scholarly research" (Lechuga and Lechuga 2012, 78).

This impetus to write reinforces habitual, and more important, workable academic writing habits even when writing is difficult. A writing faculty approach of accepting the writing process as challenging and treating writing times as pleasurable interludes directly contrasts with faculty development imperatives imploring faculty to write quickly and "get it over with." These attitudes suggest our disciplinary knowledge about writing contributes to intrinsic satisfaction from the writing process. Such satisfaction propels the interviewees to pursue writing even when another faculty meeting or committee work project threatens writing time. Though not the focus of this project, satisfaction with the writing process clearly carries over to non-academic writing projects as evidenced from Duane Roen's daily journaling practice with his wife, Malea Powell's romance novel writing, and Jonathan Alexander's creative writing projects, discussions which all worked their way into interviews about academic writing. These interviewees are administrators and editors, yet their central identities as writers have helped them continue to write for both academic and personal projects despite the additional workload. Writing faculty aren't only writing because they want to, but because they need to: "I think writing is in my DNA" (Yancey, this collection).

Writing Techniques for Process, Product, and Productivity

They Think Rhetorically (Process)

Writing faculty "think rhetorically" at the start of a writing project to determine potential audience, existing conversation on the issue, structure of writing, and mode of delivery. As Jonathan Alexander surmises in his interview, "It seems very useful to just to think rhetorically. To whom do I want to talk and how do I want to talk to them?" Malea Powell notes she starts academic pieces with this similar foundation: "Here are four things I want to say. Here are the moves I'm going to make." In their interviews, Jessica Enoch and Dànielle DeVoss likewise describe how they regularly engage in rhetorical thinking to see how a new writing project fits into an existing conversation and locate potential publication spaces where that conversation happens. In early writing process stages, for these writing faculty thinking about a potential audience means talking with potential audience members and sharing early writing with that audience to participate in the conversation on an issue. Deliberately considering the audience first counteracts expressivist advice from the field to ignore audience when starting to write. In his manifesto "Closing My Eyes as I Speak" Peter Elbow claims audience awareness often "disturbs or disrupts our writing or thinking" and writers should write to discover what they want to say without limitations (Elbow 1987, 51). Some faculty development literature supports this position as fear of audience response is cited as a frequent contributor to writer's block for academics (Hardré 2013; Kasper 2013). Yet, as Jessica Enoch advises in this collection, considering audience at the start of a project does not have to be a limiting endeavor and is often a useful method to start writing:

> Jack Selzer told me in graduate school to imagine your essays like a conversation. You know you're not competing against someone but just try to add to the conversation. I think that takes a lot of the pressure off in terms of saying that every essay has to be this groundbreaking text. Instead how can you just contribute in a smart way to a conversation you're really interested in?

This shared pattern of thinking rhetorically reveals one way writing faculty are productive. They tend to write about a central (if unfocused) idea as a starting point which helps determine (or re-determine) audience, mode, and focus. In other words, writing faculty have a sense of direction when starting.

Once writing moves from the process to the drafted product stage, interviewees commonly share writing with likely readers who may eventually serve as manuscript reviewers, a strategy also advised by faculty development literature (Carnell et al. 2008). Therefore, they go beyond thinking rhetorically to taking action in the early process stage as well. For example, both Jessica Enoch and Howard Tinberg argue early feedback from likely readers increases chances of publication because this is the audience who will read the article or cite the project when it is published (Thrower 2012), and audience awareness is essential to developing a quality publication and one of the reasons an article is published (Belcher 2009; Thrower 2012). The interviewees' responses show that writing faculty work carefully to understand the audience at the earliest writing stages. Sharing writing with colleagues also models peer response, a valued component of composition pedagogy. Peer feedback provided prior to submission to a journal strengthens the quality of the contribution and sharpens the focus on the potential audience—factors which increase a manuscript's chance at publication. An additional benefit of using peer response to think rhetorically is that readers who view prepublication drafts will know about the research and possibly want to cite the finished work—giving added incentive to the faculty writer to complete it.

They Use Invention Strategies that Foreground Discovery and Organization (Product)

Along with establishing rhetorical concerns such as audience and mode, writing faculty begin writing using two primary types of invention strategies, often simultaneously: writing to discover (sometimes called writing to learn) and outlining/scaffolding. Donald Murray (1984) considered writing a tool to uncover key ideas and careful revision of writing as a means to clarify those ideas. His writing to learn approach is already used successfully in faculty development efforts within our field such as the National Writing Project and the Bard College Institute for Writing and Thinking, and interviewees here model similar principles. In his interview, Duane Roen notes how writing to discover solves the question of where to start:

> One of the most challenging parts for me is to find out exactly where I want to go in the piece of writing so there is a little of that writing to discover, that Don Murray thing. But a lot of it is writing to discover in very rough prose composed of fragments and bullet items. Then once I know where I want to go with this chapter or article everything starts to fall into place. Once I have that rough outline I have a better feeling of where I want to go.

A key difference in Roen's writing to discover approach versus freewriting (a stream of consciousness outpouring of writing) is that Roen is simultaneously organizing his discoveries into bullets and scaffolding the frame, which helps the piece take shape. Melanie Yergeau, Cindy Selfe, and Joe Harris follow a similar strategy of establishing an early structure even if it changes as the piece develops. In other words, writing faculty are already thinking about an end product. Consistent with Roen, Yergeau writes in small idea fragments and organizes them using Scrivener concept mapping software, "so even though I still am writing in bits and pieces, which is in some ways problematic, it actually works from an outlining perspective." And when starting, Selfe asks "What's going to be the super structuring, sub-structuring, and how are these pieces related, and am I giving my audience the cues that they need in order to see the structure that I've composed for them?" and establishes an overarching framework or scaffold based on these answers as she writes.

Though outlining is criticized for being the opposite of freewriting or writing to learn due to its hierarchically-based containment structure (Crowley 2010), this consistent pattern among interviewees suggests that these successful faculty writers rely on the balance between the freedom of writing to learn and more structured techniques that scaffold and prioritize information as ideas develop. In other words, writing faculty are constantly thinking about how to organize information for a final product even when still exploring initial ideas. For example, Harris summarizes how a product-focused mindset helps structure his writing: "I start with the end, with the insight, with the point that I want to make in the end," and that paragraph moves "further and further down the page" once he adds more information to support his argument. These interviews indicate that writing faculty work to organize a writing piece even in its earliest stages, which may help lead them more rapidly to a thesis and overall structure. One of the top reasons a piece is rejected from scholarly publication is that the writing is unclear or disorganized (Belcher 2009). Having both a central idea and a structure makes it easier for writing faculty (and future journal readers) to envision the piece as an eventual publication.

They Use "Quick Focus" in Small Writing Times (Productivity)

Though most interviewees write almost every day, such regular writing only happens in brief stints. Eleven of the fifteen writers featured mentioned specifically writing in open "moments," "pockets," and "interstices" of the day. While several faculty do write at a set time each day (Alexander, Enoch, Rickert, and Roen) as writing advice guides advocate, have dedicated writing days (Powell), or occasionally binge write (Alexander, Rickert, and Yancey), writing in small moments during the day (even in five minutes) is the norm for most interviewees. One of the most compelling findings of this collection is that in a lot of ways writing faculty *don't* write in set times or blocks each day the way faculty writing guides advocate and still manage to be productive. Due to the time strapped nature of our disciplinary work, odds are stacked against writing faculty for having a dedicated block of writing time, though research has shown these do work (Boice 1990; Webber 2011). The interviewees recognize that writing projects seldom happen in isolation from other spaces of academic life such as teaching, serving on committees, and preparing for accreditation visits and must frequently jump between academic writing and other university duties. The language they use to move between projects differs, but the process is surprisingly similar. Dànielle DeVoss describes this process of flipping between projects as "toggling," a term often described when computer users switch among applications or screens. Jonathan Alexander describes it as "layering," with deliberately overlapping projects at different points in the writing process. Chris Anson describes moving between projects during the work day as "shuttling."

Even writers who block out a certain time to write each day describe toggling between writing projects or between a draft and other work such as writing a lecture, in a single day, or toggle only as they tire of one writing project and want to move to another. Though Duane Roen tends to work on a single project at a set time when possible, he also "jumps around" within singular large projects such as a textbook. Here he describes a typical scenario: "This morning I might wake up and decide that I want to work on this section of this chapter and then later in the day I might decide that I want to work on another section. My mind gets a little weary working on a section, then I do a load of laundry, let's say, and that perks me up because just changing to that new section refreshes me."

Though waiting for open moments may look like a haphazard way to write, Anson argues for toggling as a productivity strategy and advocates for leaving windows open for various projects and advises writers to "leave [a writing project] there so there's a constant reminder that there's a project waiting for your attention." DeVoss also notes this behavior works for her claiming, "I have usually 15, 16 apps open on my computer, and I just toggle between projects all day."

My interview findings confirm a pair of recent *Chronicle of Higher Education* pieces that argue writing must be done in extremely short time bursts due to the typical schedule of many academics for it to happen at all (Jenkins 2014; Semenza 2014). Notably, faculty development research provides little to no guidance as to how faculty can write productively during these small segments though more demanding faculty schedules illustrate this knowledge is badly needed (Howard 2015; Jenkins 2014; Wilson 2010). While productivity guides typically advocate for daily writing sessions of at least a half hour to two hours a day (Belcher 2009; Boice 1985, 1990; Rockquemore and Laszloffy 2008), the reality is some faculty do have an hour a day but it is scattered into ten- and fifteen-minute intervals, requiring the toggling that writing faculty describe. How faculty can make best use of these intervals and get restarted quickly is rarely described in faculty writing research, in contrast to the detail provided by the interviewees. Consider this example by Cindy Selfe, who describes how she makes small writing times work:

> None of us anymore have long, leisurely, uninterrupted days to write . . . so much of my writing is done in these small little moments of the day . . . Ten minutes, five minutes, you know two minutes, depending on what I'm writing. In between a student conference and a committee meeting, in between a class that I have to teach and my yoga exercise. There are all these demands in our day, so if I can't use these small times or interstices of my day . . . then the projects don't get done.

Though interviewees express longing for larger blocks of time for writing, they have adjusted to working in any available time, including a few stolen minutes during the work day, by using a method of quick focus as they toggle between projects.

Because writing faculty lack time to leisurely reorient themselves to a project, they restart projects quickly during these available moments (after a class, or meeting, or a student conference); a strategy Jackie Royster calls "quick focus." She claims this habit has allowed her to use whatever writing time she has, arguing, "if I've got one morning, I have to find a way to quick focus. If I've got a day on a weekend, I have to find a way to quick focus so I'm so intently focused on what I'm doing that I try to make whatever progress I can make." As one example of a way to quick focus, Dànielle DeVoss, Cindy Selfe, and Chris Anson argue for keeping writing projects on screen and returning to them often during the day even just to tweak a sentence, add a reference, or reread a difficult section to let it percolate before a meeting. This practice prevents long stretches before the writing is worked on again and saves faculty writers time needed to reorient themselves to a project, increasing overall productivity. Otherwise, as Anson notes, "I've learned that if you leave a project open on the screen and never either minimize it or put it away in a folder, whenever you open up the computer to do something else that piece is sitting staring at you, and as soon as you put it away, as soon as you put it into a folder, it's gone, and you have to force yourself to go reopen it. So, it can be gone for days." Selfe uses quick focus by deliberately ending a writing session with something enjoyable to do:

> I always try and leave writing at a point where I know what the next step is going to be so I always come back saying, "Oh, this is the point where I was going to pick up" and I always try and leave [a project] so it's like a positive thing that I want to do. You know, "Here's something I really want to do, so, oh good I get to do that!"

Selfe also stops when she knows exactly what to do next upon returning to writing (i.e., caption a video). This technique is another means to quick focus as no time is wasted figuring out how to start again. Leaving a writing session with a sense of enjoyment and a clear sense of direction for the next writing session helps maintain a sense of forward momentum necessary to engage in academic writing (Boice 1990; Boice and Jones 1984; Elbow 1987; Mayrath 2008).

As another example of a quick focus technique, Anson uses a method he calls a "semi-drafting" process where he freewrites but inserts ideas in brackets that potentially interrupt the flow as a way of recognizing them but leaving them in a safe place for later. He then keeps writing in the short blocks of time available. Anson is able to get restarted quickly because, as he notes, "I'm actually trying to write the text, but it also has all these sort of interpellations with my commentary that are the semi part, that are the 'maybe you need to do this' or 'what if you do?' . . . it's sort of an ongoing commentary to myself . . . It makes the writing feel a little bit less like you're under pressure."

Leaving notes within his draft also has the added bonus of leaving him a map of where to start when he comes back to the draft the next time as these bracketed areas can be starting points for the next writing session. In this example, Anson is writing to discover, but at the same time he doesn't forget the steps he needs to take that emerge through discovery process. Cheryl Glenn uses a similar strategy particularly when faced with interruptions during a writing session. She notes when her students come in to her office, she'll say "Just let me finish this sentence and let me write down what I was going to say next" and have them wait for a minute. She returns to writing using these notes to get started again.

Here disciplinary practices confirm research that short bursts of regular writing (Belcher 2009; Boice 1985, 1990; Elbow 1987; Hayot 2014; Rockquemore and Laszloffy 2008) indeed are necessary to move writing forward. As Elbow explains, "The productive scholar is in the habit of writing, at least notes, at least lists, at least fragmentary drafts, at least something that keeps the topic alive and growing so that writing will come that is ready to be written" (Elbow 1987, 148). Repeated contact with the writing helps the writer to restart quickly because less time is needed to revisit where writing was left off. Though toggling or shuttling between projects is not the model typically advocated by faculty development resources, it has the added benefit of fitting flexibly within the open moments for writing in combination with the quick focus method of writing in small time periods that writing faculty have adapted to.

As these patterns illustrate, instead of working with a vague "big idea," rhetoric and writing faculty work quickly to sort through the noise around the big idea and organize to set a clear path as they write. A clear path, even if it is revised as writing progresses, helps faculty work deliberately through various scattered and small writing sessions. Faculty development research indicates getting restarted after several days of not writing is extremely difficult and one of the most common reasons faculty don't write (Belcher 2009; Boice 1990; Hardré 2013). The technique of quick focus, combined with the techniques of thinking rhetorically and using invention strategies to discover and scaffold information in concert, help writing faculty members combat the impulse to make circular versus forward progress on their writing projects. This is particularly important when writing faculty are often writing in short, fragmented bursts on most days.

HOW TO USE THIS BOOK

The patterns for analysis described above are a useful starting point for any researcher wanting to look at specific trends among writing faculty habits. Yet this collection of interviews offers additional openings for rhetoric and composition scholars to use the findings as writing advice for various points in a career. In this spirit of opportunity, I envision four ways readers might use *How Writing Faculty Write* and describe potential applications below.

For Graduate Students Entering the Discipline

Advice is often given to graduate students to establish writing habits that will serve them well as future faculty, but research has shown we don't yet do this. Laura Micciche described her graduate experience as a rhetoric and composition student learning to write for an academic career as a stressful one, noting " . . . so overwhelmed we were by all that we had to know in order to create writing that made a contribution, no matter how minor, or just made sense" (Micciche and Carr 2011, 479). The "complexity of becoming socialized into a field of inquiry" frequently contributes to the struggle Micciche describes—to get words on the page as a writer grapples with a new field or new subject for an article. Reframing this same struggle as a requisite part of the scholarly inquiry necessary to write (Scott 2014, 65), as writing faculty do, allows movement beyond writing blocks. More specifically, threaded through discussions are descriptions of how to start projects and how to revise writing both speak directly about how to become an academic writer versus how to get published, a conversation lacking in rhetoric and composition graduate education (Micciche and Carr 2011; Soderlund 2015; Wells 2015). Keeping this gap in mind, I'd urge graduate student readers to pay attention to two specific conversations on starting projects and revising that will serve them well regardless of the type of institution they end up at as faculty.

As a faculty developer as well as a rhetoric and composition faculty member, I regularly work with new faculty who are not sure how to start a new project once they have exhausted all publication and presentation possibilities from dissertation work. As a group, writing faculty think rhetorically to get started as noted in the "Patterns for Analysis" section above. But they also get started using a variety of concrete strategies graduate students can observe from interviews from Dànielle DeVoss who begins drafting a future publication onsite with her conference panel at a professional conference, Joe Harris who uses research on student writing from his classroom as an entry point, Kathi Yancey who uses slides as an invention technique after learning something new, or Thomas Rickert who describes how he starts with web searching to begin a multimedia project.

As revision strategies are notoriously difficult to teach students and something unlikely that graduate students pick up in their programs (Micciche and Carr 2011; Soderlund 2015; Wells 2015), they also need multiple models of how publishing writing faculty are moving from a draft to a publishable final product. In his interview, Chris Anson refers to revision as a craft and makes the argument for how writing studies as a field values good academic writing: "I like writers who really craft their writing. I think too often we forget as compositionists, we want to be writing really well in addition to researching well." In her analysis of *Studies of Higher Education* articles, Helen Sword (2009) finds that though most academics claim to prefer reading academic articles that are well crafted, only six of the fifty articles she analyzed had well-crafted sentences. Echoing the findings from the interviewees who work to develop well-crafted writing, Sword argues, "We owe it to our colleagues, our students, our institutions and, yes, to ourselves to write as the most effective teachers teach: with passion, with craft, with care and with style" (Sword 2009, 334). Revision not only increases the chances of publication because the writing is better organized and developed but also ensures that the product demonstrates high quality writing that Anson notes scholars in the field of writing should strive for. Though most of the interviews discuss revision, wonderfully detailed conversations on various revision processes can be found in interviews with Harris, Rickert, and Yancey.

For New Faculty and Novice Scholars Thinking about Their Writing Lives

At this early career stage, productive writing habits become essential to publishing regularly for tenure, career advancement, and/or employment mobility. Two conversations are especially useful here—time management strategies based on life stages and the importance of building a publishing network. As new rhetoric and composition faculty make the transition from graduate school into full-time faculty positions, most realize that open blocks of writing time they may have had as students no longer exist and/or binge writing episodes to get dissertation chapters completed won't function in a new faculty position when teaching early classes. Though some graduate students already regularly navigate an intense schedule, for example working students or those juggling child or elder care responsibilities, many new faculty come to find the realities of teaching a 4–4 load with high service expectations and possible writing program administrative work leaves little time for writing. It is here the interviews are most useful as models for these readers based on circumstance. Working parents might find interviews by Enoch, Rickert, and Royster helpful as all three address balancing work and families. Those with 4–4 loads or otherwise jam-packed schedules can see how different attempts at carving up writing times into specific segments of the day such as early mornings (Alexander, Roen, Enoch) or, more randomly, in small interstices of the day (Anson, DeVoss, Selfe) help writing faculty make forward progress.

A second thread of conversation for new faculty to follow is how networks are built among writing faculty, which contributes to a pipeline of publication opportunity. Faculty featured here continually publish because new projects are constantly thrown their way. An acquaintance will develop an edited collection or textbook and ask interviewees interested in the same area to contribute (DeVoss, Roen). Others will talk after a conference panel, meet potential collaborators, and make plans to develop a project (DeVoss). Still others maintain relationships with their graduate students once those students move on to become colleagues and work on future publications (Blair). The message here is that writing faculty are not (only) holing up in their offices trying to write alone. While initially they may focus on solo-authored scholarship to get tenure (see Yergeau, who describes navigating this process) they are also building connections and networks that foster new projects in the future. Such networking ensures a steady workflow, particularly because rhetoric and composition is a collaborative field.

For Mid-Level/Senior Faculty Wanting to Know More about How These Scholars Work and Write

While the secret writing lives of colleagues featured in *How Writing Faculty Write* might be an initial draw, the interviews offer advice for effective collaborative writing, managing multiple projects, mentoring other writers, and choosing projects later in a career.

Many famous writing pairs within the field rhetoric and composition exist (Ede and Lunsford, Flower and Hayes, Hawisher and Selfe, etc.), and collaborative writing is a valued practice in the field. Earlier research within the field describes successful collaborations (Ede and Lunsford 1990; Haswell and Haswell 2010; Yancey and Spooner 1998), and interview findings build on these, offering a deeper look at how collaboratively produced writing gets started, exchanged, and revised. For Kathi Yancey, asking pointed and specific questions about how a collaboration will function lays out the map to finishing a writing task:

> How are you going to start? Is one of you going to draft one section, another of you is going to draft a different section, then you're going to swap? Or is somebody going to do basically a concept and then another person is going to take that concept and run with it and then swap it back and forth? When you swap back and forth are you going to use track changes [in Microsoft Word] or are you going to give people permission to overwrite your prose and you won't know where they changed it?

To learn how writing faculty answer these questions, Blair's interview on writing with graduate students stands out here, as do interviews by Enoch, Selfe, and Roen who offer specific strategies for writing effectively with colleagues, describing everything from how to actually exchange the writing to how to navigate the blending of voices.

Mid-level and senior faculty take on more work and have to manage multiple writing projects. Several faculty have developed systems that work for tracking projects from idea to published artifact that these faculty may find helpful as models. The big picture perspective helps writing faculty see what is completed and how much work can be done at any given time. Organizing writing projects is essential to make sure that projects get completed (Goodsen 2012), and having an organization system is even more crucial when working on projects in fragments. Chris Anson makes "grids" to track projects as well as map writing time, a habit he started as an assistant professor: "I started making these grids that tracked projects from either an early idea or a conference paper all the way through to eventual publication. I started filling these grids out thinking, 'I've got to keep pushing each of these things forward until it gets out in print,' and these also served as maps for writing days." Interviews with Anson, Alexander, and DeVoss all describe effective methods for organizing multiple projects.

Beyond effective organization techniques, interviews from senior leaders discuss how having passion for projects and strategies for cultivating passion is essential once tenure has been achieved. As a group, the interviewees are not as interested in getting published as in the work they are publishing, and this attitude may come with more experience in the field. As a result, post-tenure they pursue projects that sustain their interest. Malea Powell sums up an attitude frequently in evidence from the interviews: "I don't want to be engaged in doing work that I think is not interesting just in order to get the next rung on the ladder." Sometimes they perform, as Thomas Rickert describes, "academic triage" and focus on saving only the writing projects worth saving even though they have multiple publication opportunities on offer. Writing faculty find passion for projects in many different ways such as sharing writing with colleagues (see Enoch, DeVoss), developing a signature writing style or methodology (see Glenn, Rickert), collaborating with students or faculty (see Blair, DeVoss, Roen), or working in mediums that are better suited to their purposes (see Powell, Rickert, Roen, Selfe, Yergeau).

A final thread senior faculty may find useful is one about mentoring. Though mentoring may not seem like it has a direct impact on writing productivity, as senior faculty describe how they mentor others, they are writing themselves. Cheryl Glenn models writing in her office while leaving the door open so graduate students can see her writing and understand it takes physical work and time dedication (i.e., writing doesn't happen mysteriously or automatically). Duane Roen explicitly teaches his graduate students "habits of mind" for writing success (see Council of Writing Program Administrators 2011) noting, "When I work with student writers, one of the things that I try to convince them is you don't have to be brilliant to be a productive writer, but you do have to have these good work habits." He then models his own work habits.

Cindy Selfe assigns "model" articles with her graduate students to not only teach them how to use academic language in an argument but also to revisit herself what makes articles effective. And Kris Blair actively works with students on her own writing projects as part of graduate instruction, building their own publication records in the process. All of these interviews are useful maps for mentoring but also offer additional strategies for writing effectively. Teaching and modeling the processes of academic writing allows interviewees to not only continue to write (and therefore keep academic writing central to daily work) but to use previously mentioned writing process strategies such as rhetorical thinking or product strategies such as collaboration simultaneously.

For Historians of Rhetoric and Composition and Metadisciplinary Scholars

Many interviewees featured here are early members of the field (Glenn, Harris, Roen, Selfe, Yancey, etc.) and as such, they provide a narrative history of how writing practices as a field have developed collectively. Despite anthologizing other corners of our field such as our journals (Goggin 2000) and our WPA practices (Enos, Borrowman, and Skeffington 2008; Ostman 2013), this is an area that more research is needed to capture. Interviews featuring discussions of landmark works such as Joe Harris's *A Teaching Subject*, Alexander's *Understanding Rhetoric*, or Glenn's *Rhetoric Retold* are a useful starting point for capturing our writing history. The interviews with field leaders also offer a look at the history of our field that has yet to be written (see Glenn's discussion of revisiting Ed Corbett's *Classical Rhetoric for the Modern Student* and Tinberg's potential memoir of working as a teaching scholar at a community college, along with other "dream projects" described by Blair, Enoch, and Harris). Moreover, with a history of computers and composition more than thirty years old, interviews offer a reflective look at what writing within the field looks like at this moment of technological impact. Interviews from Blair, DeVoss, Selfe, and Yergeau all describe writing process tensions that rhetoric and composition scholars currently navigate when publishing in both print and digital mediums.

Looking ahead to the interviews featured here, there have been calls to do *Review*-style projects asking about faculty writing practices. In 1986, Murray invited rhetoric and composition faculty to "reveal their own craft [of writing] so those who join our profession can become productive members of it—and share the secret pleasure in writing which we feel but rarely admit" (146). In one of the only open discussions of faculty writing within writing studies, he described specific methods for prewriting, drafting, and publishing. In the process, Murray revealed tidbits such as the fact that he used a planning notebook to write in small fragments of time and that many of his articles had a five-year publication timeline due to an incubation process where he occasionally stopped writing to think about ideas. That same year, Maxine Hairston issued a similar call and invited writing teachers to share how they write with faculty colleagues and students. To model this process, she revealed that she experienced the "imposter syndrome" after receiving an advance contract for a book and struggled to write (Hairston 1986). These first models of how writing faculty might talk about writing for publication echo the ways *Review* interviewees talked openly about the "back story" of the real writing processes behind famous pieces, and the conversations ahead are similarly honest and enlightening. Though a reader's guide is offered above, interviews, or parts of interviews, can be read in any order.

Let's get the conversation started.

1

CYNTHIA SELFE

CYNTHIA L. SELFE is, in her words, "blissfully retired." A former humanities distinguished professor in the Department of English at The Ohio State University and founder and previous co-editor of *Computers and Composition: An International Journal*, Selfe has a prolific publishing record. To date she has published both print and digital form, four single authored books, a co-authored book, ten edited collections, nineteen book chapters, and sixty-five journal articles. In 2007, Selfe co-founded the Computers and Composition Digital Press.

Selfe has served as the chair of the national Conference on College Composition and Communication and the chair of the College Section of the National Council of Teachers of English and held a variety of administrative roles. In 2014, Selfe won the Conference on College Composition and Communication's Exemplar Award.

Selfe began her career at Michigan Technological University, a science and engineering focused institution of seven thousand students located in the Upper Peninsula, and worked there for twenty-four years before taking a position at Ohio State. Along the way, she taught courses in computers including Hypertext Theory and Computers and Writing, composition, scientific and technical communication, and literature, including a course titled Literature and Lore of the Upper Peninsula, among others. Over the course of her career, she has served in a variety of administrative positions including chair of the English Department and director of the writing center at Michigan Tech. Selfe's interview took place on May 19, 2013, in her office at Ohio State University.

CHRISTINE: Why aren't we studying ourselves as writers? We've studied ourselves as teachers, we've studied ourselves as activists, as literate beings through the DALN [Digital Archive of Literacy Narratives], but when we're talking about our actual writing for publication, the stuff we need to do to keep our jobs, why aren't we talking about that?

CINDY: I think it's a wonderful question. I think that part of the response there is that scholars of rhetoric and composition are supposed to

DOI: 10.7330/9781607326625.c001

be able to write. I think that's the expectation, that we have not only as writing our subject matter, our disciplinary subject matter and the subject matter that we teach, but that we have some facility with language itself and the writing of language and the articulation of ideas through written language as part of being a professor of rhetoric and composition.

CHRISTINE: Agreed.

CINDY: That said, while I believe that's an expectation, I don't think that's always a reality. In fact, I know colleagues struggle a great deal with composing and writing their scholarly work. I certainly do. I mean, I slog through my scholarly work. I only write when I get so uncomfortable with having to write, that I really have to get down to it, and once I get down to it it's not as awful as I remember it. But it is a slow, hard, slog through materials, collecting the materials, doing the research if I'm doing the research or finding the scholarly sources and then fitting them together in a way that makes sense to me, and then the way that makes sense to me is never the way that I know editors are going to like it so I have to adapt it to my audience, my editorial audience, my audience of colleagues.

CHRISTINE: I see.

CINDY: To complicate that, I guess I have gotten dissatisfied with alphabetic writing as a venue for that kind of articulation. I've really have gotten dissatisfied with the flatness of alphabetic writing and so now I can't even start writing until I also start thinking of how it's going to look, what is the design going to be. What's the platform in which I'm going to explore these ideas? Is it going to be a web based text or a Prezi, or is it going to be a blog or comic? Not only the medium, but the modalities of expression and the genre are dimensions I have to figure out in terms of the composing that I do. So composing is not an easy task for me.

CHRISTINE: Even now.

CINDY: Especially now. Especially now because there are so many more choices and expectations of course, both mine and people who read the work that I do. There are a lot of layers to consider.

CHRISTINE: Can you give an example?

CINDY: I was composing a presentation for the Computers and Writing conference about sound. I had to figure out not only how I was going to compose the alphabetic portion of the presentation but also how I was going to present that presentation using Keynote or PowerPoint. Then I had to identify how I was going to show some video clips. And then I had to think about how I was going to caption those video clips to make sure that they were accessible.

CHRISTINE: There are multiple issues with invention here.

CINDY: *Then* part of the talk was about an audio portion of those video clips so I had to figure out how to use a program that did a screen capture of the .wav form as it played and highlighted specific parts of that .wav form as it played so that the sound, the video, the attention to the specific points of the .wav form would be evident for the audience while I did the talking. That layering of semiotic channels for the kinds of concepts I want to convey when I write are becoming more complex. For that reason, I think that composition is both more interesting and more challenging.

CHRISTINE: I was looking at some of your recent work on sound, and I did find it sort of ironic that this really cool piece ["The Movement of Air, the Breath of Meaning: Aurality and Multimodal Composing"] was out there, the one you just did in one of our flagship journals; it's such a cool piece . . .

CINDY: It's all in print.

CHRISTINE: It's all in print. Because it was a sound piece as a reader I expected voice. Somehow you did manage to convey that audio aspect in print, but there is a challenge . . .

CINDY: . . . The challenge was when that piece was put in our flagship journal, the three C's [*College Composition and Communication*] . . .

CHRISTINE: Three C's, let's mention it.

CINDY: Right, let's mention it, three C's! That was before they had an online presence and one of the things that I told the editors was that I can write this piece about sound but readers would have to go to the sound pieces themselves in order to listen to them in order to understand what I'm saying about this piece. We had to come up with a very strange solution by writing about sound and then linking to online sources.

CHRISTINE: A compromise.

CINDY: It wasn't the last piece I'll write, but I think it's going to be one of the last pieces I actually publish that's flat like that, because I can't write about the things that I want to write about without including video and audio in the piece itself. The most recent piece that I've published that I'm happiest with is a digital book [*Stories that Speak to Us*] and that digital book has video, and audio, and links, and dimension for me that the piece in the three C's simply didn't have, and couldn't, at the time that it was written. Things have changed pretty fast.

CHRISTINE: I heard that from one of your interviews [in *Women's Ways of Making It in Rhetoric and Composition*] that you wrote in "interstices" of your day . . .

CINDY: I do.

CHRISTINE: Can you describe that process a little bit more? That was the coolest part of that interview for me as a time strapped writing program administrator.

CINDY: I do; it's absolutely the truth. I mean, none of us anymore have long, leisurely, uninterrupted days to write . . . so much of my writing is done in these small little moments of the day.

CHRISTINE: How small?

CINDY: Ten minutes, five minutes, you know two minutes, depending on what I'm writing. In between a student conference and a committee meeting, in between a class that I have to teach and my yoga exercise. There's all these demands in our day, so if I can't use these small times or interstices of my day, exactly as you say, then the projects don't get done.

CHRISTINE: So true.

CINDY: One of the habits I've developed as a writer is making my writing very modular so I always think of my thesis. I have to think of that first, and then I have four or five parts of that argument and then I start on part one, and in part one I probably will have three or four parts of that so I just do it part by part by part and then eventually I will stitch those parts together. If I make it small enough I can work on the little parts in the time I have. I figure "Oh, I have to do this video" so that is the little part that I work on in the first ten minutes, or twenty minutes, or half hour or whatever of my day. If I do all those little parts every single day, soon enough I turn around and there's a collection of parts that I can put together and that makes the whole. But I have to field the work on little pieces like that.

CHRISTINE: How do you do it? I see how that process would work when starting off the day and after a meeting or an expected writing break, but once so many things that happen in a day, how do you get yourself focused again to get back to writing?

CINDY: Here's one thing I do. I always try and leave writing at a point where I know what the next step is going to be so I always come back saying, "Oh, this is the point where I was going to pick up" and I always try and leave [a project] so it's like a positive thing that I want to do. You know, "Here's something I really want to do, so, oh good I get to do that!" I get to do that part now where I caption a video so it's something I know how to do and it's something I know where I'm going to go with it and I always try and stop at a point where I can go on with it pretty easily, I can jump back into it pretty easily. I also like to write while I'm doing other things. I will write a lot when I'm watching TV and I'll write, I write during faculty meetings.

CHRISTINE: Don't tell anybody, I do it too! [laughs]

CINDY: I love to write during faculty meetings or do sort of mindless things, like if there's indexing or something small to do that, I can pay attention and do it at the same time.

CHRISTINE: How does your composing process work when you collaborate? You collaborate with a lot of people.

CINDY: I've seen people that collaborate that sit down together and discuss, discuss, discuss. I'm not that kind of collaborator. The kind of collaboration I like is where I do everything that I can to do the piece and then I hand it off and I know somebody else is working on it and they're doing a great job. I totally give it over. I don't care if they change every single one of my blessed words as long as they're doing something and moving the piece forward. That's how Gail and I have developed the habit of working and I just assume she is constantly making that piece better when it's out of my hands.

CHRISTINE: It's a famous writing relationship.

CINDY: . . . which is why I love to collaborate, because when it's off my desk I can be doing something else and trusting that she is doing the work on that one. So often we're working on two or three pieces at a time and we're trading them back and forth. But we only go back and forth maybe three or four times at the maximum because we really do write, most of the piece like whoever is writing it first will write most of the piece. We'll leave some big hunks undone that the other one will have to do, or the other person is in charge of making it richer and more dimensional, but we just hand it over. So I like working with somebody but only somebody who will take it up. The kind of people I really don't like working with will track changes and ask all these questions. I'd rather them do the work, just go ahead and do it.

CHRISTINE: Commit to the writing and be sure! [laughs]

CINDY: Yes, just go ahead and make the changes! Then, let's read the text and see if the text makes sense. I'm not protective of my words. I want [writing collaborators] to actually mix it [the text] up with me in there. I don't want to be able to point to something and be like "That's my paragraph" or "That's my idea." I would rather not. Right now, honestly if somebody asked me which parts of this work or that work were Gail's and which parts were mine . . . I wouldn't know.

CHRISTINE: So the patches are hidden and you can't see that spot where you splice your writing efforts together?

CINDY: The only way I can tell is if we're writing about the students at Illinois or the students at Ohio State because I know those students, so I know who did the initial writing about that but many times the work is very close together.

CHRISTINE: I don't think there's a way that we could have an interview about rhetoric and composition without talking about the teaching piece because so much of what we do in rhetoric and composition is tied to teaching. Are you able to convey your own writing habits to your students?

CINDY: Well, you came in on one of the conversations [laughs] . . .

CHRISTINE: I did, that's what gave me the idea. [laughs]

CINDY: When you came into my office I was talking to Will Kurlinkus, a graduate student who is just getting ready to do his dissertation and he was thinking about what form is this dissertation going to take. Now that we have these [technology] options we need to think rhetorically about what we're trying to accomplish, what the content demands, the genre demands, the audience demands, how we want to present ourselves as authors and as scholars, and on the job market. For him, this is his move into a scholarly arena.

CHRISTINE: And you guide him toward these rhetorical choices?

CINDY: All of those questions that I keep asking myself, I hope that I help students ask the same kinds of questions. I hope what I pass along to them is that they don't have to be limited only to print unless they think print is right for a particular piece, for a particular audience, for a particular journal and makes ideas accessible to the people who are doing the reading. I hope that I pass along to graduate students I work with that sense of possibility of different mediums, modalities of expression, and the demands of genre, audience, authorship, identity. Remember when we were talking about structure and writing in interstices and breaking things down into small enough things? I'm big on structure. As I think about a project I like to think in terms of, "Okay how am I going to structure this piece, what's going to be the super structuring, sub-structuring, and how are these pieces related, and am I giving my audience the cues that they need in order to see the structure that I've composed for them?"

CHRISTINE: So organization is always a priority when you are teaching about writing?

CINDY: Organization is huge with me and I'd like to think that I pass along to students that kind of eye for organization and structure rather than simply letting a piece happen. I don't believe in letting a piece happen. Instead I point out there's a structure that you've got in your head for your argument or your writing and to make that manifest, to build that structure for yourself and then to make it evident and manifest for a readership.

CHRISTINE: Particularly with doctoral students, I'm thinking of a dissertation, for many of them, will be the longest thing they will have written up until that point so it is easy to lose the throughline.

CINDY: It is.

CHRISTINE: Or to just rely on chapters as the organizational structure, but that's not necessarily the best way to think about it.

CINDY: Exactly, so that structuring and organization is *huge* for me. Also the arrangement is key because the arrangement is how you make manifest that structure and organization for an audience. I just taught a class on writing for publication, and I think I have a fairly rhetorical understanding of publication venues. We do a lot of analysis of what kinds of audiences and journals we're writing for and who reads those journals whether they're online or in print. We look at what they require and value. In teaching I ask "Are there other pieces within the journal or within the genre that you can point to that will help you structure and explore your own piece?" I use a lot of modelers.

CHRISTINE: Model articles?

CINDY: Absolutely. Either the article may be a model in terms of its content or in terms of its organization or in terms of its design or on any other terms. I'm huge on models. So, we did a little bit of that in the publication class. I also love style. Rhetorical style is very important to me and so I ask students a lot to look at their language and to see how they're using language to make claims, to provide evidence, to identify themselves as a researcher, to formulate an identity as a scholar.

CHRISTINE: A difficult task.

CINDY: You know, all language is political and the way that they write passes along information about the kind of scholar they are. So I'm huge on making . . . how do I put this nicely? I think that some scholars write in a way that is purposefully obfuscating by trying to be scholarly and by trying to be richly textured in their understandings of works and people. I think that sometimes writers don't focus on being politically accessible to different kinds of readers. We could do a lot with that use of style to make ideas elegant and elegantly accessible to a lot of readers. I think that's a requirement for me. The style is a political statement of how I want my scholarship to be.

CHRISTINE: It does seem that some students seem to feel that if an academic article is accessible it must not be intellectual and those styles are totally opposite.

CINDY: Exactly, I think people sometimes mistake the elegant simplicity that I'm after for a simplicity of ideas and that's not the case. I want really complex ideas elegantly stated so that they're accessible to the broadest number of people.

CHRISTINE: You've mentioned retirement.

CINDY: [laughs] Yeah.

CHRISTINE: [laughs] You look very happy about it.

CINDY: I am, I am.

CHRISTINE: What do you think is going to happen for you in terms of your writing?

CINDY: I have no idea. I do think I will continue composing texts in some way. One of the things that I am sorry for in my career is that I'm a bit of a one trick pony. Most of the writing or composing that I do takes the form of scholarly articles and that's a limited and limiting genre in some sense for me. I wish I had learned how to compose other things. I would like to be a novelist, I would like to be a short story writer, I would like to be able to write for the public in other ways like for *The Nation*, or for *The Chronicle* or something but I just don't do it. Partially because I don't think I have time and partially because I haven't studied that genre enough and I need to study the genres before I can write. I would like to think I'll be composing texts for other venues and genres when I retire.

CHRISTINE: Do you have any final advice for faculty that are struggling with writing?

CINDY: I think [writing is] very idiosyncratic. Some of the problems with giving advice about writing is that it has to work in your day, in your time, you have to be excited about doing it, not me, and what excites me is not going to excite you or anybody else. What I would say to people who want to be academic writers is to find out what excites you first, and then write about the kind of stuff that excites you, rather than thinking of the fact that you have to do this writing. I would say find stuff that you really want to compose about, things that you have something to say about, things that you think are important, things that you have to offer and then you will be more likely to want do the composing.

CHRISTINE: Anything else regarding motivation?

CINDY: Find something that is as fun as possible for you to do. Multimodal composing for me is fun because it is very satisfying to arrange and rearrange and to compose and create in multiple layers and then to arrange these layers in ways that are thoughtful and meaningful for me. I keep writing because that kind of composing and arranging and organizing is very satisfying and fun for me. When writers find meaningful topics that are satisfying for them, it's much easier to pursue writing because there is something now to say.

2

JOSEPH HARRIS

JOSEPH HARRIS is an English professor at the University of Delaware, where he teaches composition, creative nonfiction, and digital writing. Before coming to Delaware, he was the founding director of the Thompson Writing Program at Duke University—a multidisciplinary program noted for teaching writing as a form of critical inquiry. His books include *Rewriting: How to Do Things with Texts*, *A Teaching Subject*, and *Teaching with Student Texts*. He has served as editor of College Composition and Communication, the leading scholarly journal in writing studies, and of the Conference on College Composition and Communication Studies in Writing and Rhetoric, the leading book series in the field. He is currently at work on a book about how the teaching of writing has been depicted in contemporary films, plays, and novels.

Harris has centered his career on mentoring new teachers of writing. During the ten years he directed the Duke writing program, he recruited over eighty postdoctoral fellows from a wide range of disciplines and guided them as they designed and taught writing-intensive seminars in their fields. Several of these postdocs now serve in leadership roles in writing programs across the country. At Delaware he advises graduate students, postdoctoral fellows, and faculty members on teaching writing, and in 2016 received the College of Arts and Sciences Award for Excellence in Service. He also works frequently with K–12 teachers of writing and language arts and is often asked to lead workshops for faculty at other universities. To find out more, visit josephharris.me. The interview took place on July 8, 2013, via Skype.

JOE: I thought it was funny to talk about writing projects today. I'm returning to writing work after spending about a month or two moving, closing down one house, opening another, gardening, that kind of stuff. If I weren't being interviewed right now, I'd be typing to try to get some writing done!

DOI: 10.7330/9781607326625.c002

CHRISTINE: **Let's start with something from past work as a launching point then. In a few of your works, you note teaching writing offers a way for writing professors to talk about writing in rhetoric and composition scholarship. Do you feel that the writing that you do as a professor and then the writing that your students do is somewhat inseparable based on your body of work?**

JOE: Let's put it this way. I consider myself a teacher of writing rather than a rhetorician or even primarily a scholar. The most direct inspiration for my work has been the work that I do with undergraduates in the classroom. That has always been the case. I find student writing really just an interesting cultural phenomenon. I like to think about it. When you are working with apprentices, they say and do things that are surprising and interesting, and yes, unpredictable. I do feel like I learn a lot both in terms of thinking about teaching and thinking about writing, but I also see changes in the actual kind of writing I do.

CHRISTINE: **How so?**

JOE: One of the things I've recently tried to do over the years is to shift my style a little bit. I try to imagine myself as writing some of my work that might be read by both undergraduates and by colleagues at the same time, and I've found that kind of writing really very rewarding.

CHRISTINE: **Your scholarship seems to pay careful attention to undergraduate writers not only as readers but also as authors. You talk a fair bit in publications, including *A Teaching Subject*, about how to use student work ethically, for example how to quote it and how to write about it in rhetoric and composition research. How do you draw that line between leading readers in the field of rhetoric and composition to what you want them to get from the student research and letting the student work speak for itself?**

JOE: I've become a little more aware of and interested in the issues around use of student work in research. I guess I've begun to see it as potentially problematic in ways that hadn't occurred to me when I first started doing it. I recently published a piece in *JAC* called "Using Student Texts in Composition Scholarship" and I talk about the challenge of using student texts a lot. In one of the postscripts in the revised version of *A Teaching Subject* I also talk about best practices for using student work.

CHRISTINE: **It is an underexplored area of research, and one I struggle to explain to graduate students looking to analyze student papers in their research.**

JOE: After writing a lot about this, I have two thoughts about how to use student work that emerge in my own writing. On the one hand, when I first started using student writing, I would basically quote pieces that interested me the way I would quote anything else. I always got permission, but it was always retrospective. I don't think I was especially cautious about using the work and no one ever refused my request to use their work, which over the long haul strikes me as slightly suspicious.

CHRISTINE: [laughs]

JOE: [laughs] I may have been benignly pressuring them more than I thought I was. Now what I do is ask students whether they'd like to be quoted by name or no, and I've been interested that some prefer not to be quoted by me. They still see student writing as sort of apprentice work basically, rather than something that that they want linked to their names for the rest of their lives. I've tried to make my citing of student work a bit more open and transparent. At the same time, I think there are some in the field who argue for, what seem to me, a fairly elaborate set of cautions and procedures. For example, in terms of citing student work, of always getting work in advance and making sure that you never cite the work of your own students—basically setting up a kind of research protocol to create and acquire the texts that you're going to work with. And while I understand that impulse, I actually think there's something limiting about it . . .

CHRISTINE: How so?

JOE: I think limitation tends to work against a use of a student text in the same way that I use articles and books by other intellectuals. When I'm thinking about a subject and wanting to cite something and I think "Oh! Didn't I read an essay about that?" and sometimes it's an essay that a fellow scholar has written or that someone in *The Atlantic* or *The New Yorker* has written, and sometimes it's actually an essay I remember reading in a, a class that I've been teaching. It's been useful for me to have those different kinds of writing in the mix, and I wouldn't want to lose that sense of, of serendipity. Having the option to treat student texts as valid sources actually has been very important to the kind of writing I do. So, I both want to allow for that kind of chance but at the same point, let the moment of actually working with the student text to be very open, very transparent.

CHRISTINE: How do you ensure that transparency happens?

JOE: I let students read the work that I cite and what I have to say about it. I talk with them to make sure that they feel good about how I have represented their writing.

CHRISTINE: You mentioned *A Teaching Subject.* You've had this unique opportunity to "rewrite yourself" and one of the landmark texts in our field through the postscripts in the new edition. Because you've worked with the concept of rewriting in *Rewriting: How to Do Things with Texts* I wondered if writing the new postscripts was a challenge because, essentially, you're in conversation with yourself.

JOE: The postscripts were more difficult to write than I thought. They're short pieces but I think I had this vision of when I first started that I could knock off each postscript in two days or something because they're only about 50 words long.

CHRISTINE: What was difficult about writing these short pieces?

JOE: They probably took two weeks rather than two days for each one. First of all, I found that I wanted to go back and read things. I wanted to think about things. And, as I always do, I ended up fussing with the length a good bit. I will say that even though it was slower and more difficult to write these, they were also pleasurable to write.

CHRISTINE: What was so satisfying?

JOE: I decided to write postscripts because I am a compulsive reviser and didn't want to change the original text. I thought that if I were going to try to rewrite the chapters that I would be doing a kind of violence to the work that I was doing in the 1990s, and what the reader would end up with was this curious book which would then be my take on composition since 1966 as of 2012 rather than 1996. I actually didn't want to erase that early work. Instead I just wanted to think about *A Teaching Subject* as a text in itself and respond to it. So that's why I decided to add the short pieces. I didn't want to replace 1996 sentences with 2012 sentences, which is what I think I would have done if I had just tried to overhaul the whole thing. I like the book as it stands—as it stood, and I wanted it to stay that way, but I also wanted to add to it.

CHRISTINE: A fresh take, I see.

JOE: Yes, I think so. I'm happy with it.

CHRISTINE: Staying on the subject of rewriting and revision, because you work in this unique space between working with student work and also being a writer yourself, do you follow your own revision advice that you give to students?

JOE: I think the answer is yes and no.

CHRISTINE: [laughs] I've heard that a lot during these interviews!

JOE: [laughs] I'm not surprised. I do think the answer is yes in that I think I ask myself the same kind of questions when I return to a text. As I suggest to students and in my writing, I really imagine much of the work of composing at the point of revision rather than the point of invention. I mean, that's where I feel more in control. That's where I take more pleasure in craft. When I'm working with other writers, revision is the moment where I feel we have something to talk about together. I do think there have been a lot of writing teachers who are very good at talking about how you get from nothing to something, from a blank page or screen to writing upon it, and I've just always thought that getting started was a matter of, you know, good luck and staring at the computer! [laughs]

CHRISTINE: [laughs]

JOE: So, I don't know that I have advice about helping writers with invention per se. It's really at the point of working with the text that I feel both that I can analyze what I'm doing and help other people do their work. I ask the same kinds of questions of myself as I do my students. I think as with any craft, a lot more of that work becomes internalized rather than on the page, and I don't think my pieces necessarily proceed in the same sort of set of drafts that my students tend to submit to me.

CHRISTINE: **Where do you think the difference lies?**

JOE: I revise a lot, but I tend to revise as I go along, and that means not only rewriting sentences after you write them but rereading the day's work . . . you know, what you wrote before, the day before and adding to it, changing it around, moving the paragraphs, and so on. And, I think I've just been doing it long enough that I don't have to write out a full draft, then write a second draft, and then write a third draft. A lot of that work goes on in my head as I'm taking my dogs for a walk and walking around the house, and so on.

CHRISTINE: **It's more seamless then a student process you would say . . . ?**

JOE: I think internalized rather than seamless. I think a lot of the discussion now goes on inside my head rather than written down on the page.

CHRISTINE: **You said when we started the interview that you had this very long break from writing?**

JOE: Yep.

CHRISTINE: **Long for you.**

JOE: [laughs]

Christine. How do you get yourself writing again?

JOE: [laughs] This is probably just a terrible answer, but just by trying to force myself to do it basically. I'm sure that other people you've interviewed have this also but getting into the flow is the most difficult part of writing for me.

CHRISTINE: **They have. I've had a lot of conversations about how to focus quickly and get started writing again because procrastination sometimes sets in.**

JOE: Moving past the point of procrastination or writer's block for me is just sitting down and starting to type. I do think, by the way, that some of that procrastination is actually something more like incubation. When I begin a project, I really have to think about it, and it takes me awhile to sort through what it is that I want to say and to think about how I want to begin and what books I want to have on my desk and so on, and that's not a particularly organized process. It's just a lot of time walking the dogs and walking around the house and thinking about the piece and thinking I should be writing, but yet for some reason not quite being able to do it.

CHRISTINE: **I think a lot of new writing faculty might wonder about this, but what motivates you to finally sit down and start typing? What actually gets you to sit in the chair?**

JOE: At a certain point, incubation has helped focus my mind usefully and I'm just ready to get started. Beyond that, deadlines are good. I try to pride myself on meeting deadlines. I don't always do so. The piece I have to write this month will be a couple of weeks late, but I've talked with the editor that [laughs] and I also use the threat of social shame to make sure I'm writing!

CHRISTINE: [laughs] Always a good motivator.

JOE: But in terms of actual tricks—like how do I start thinking about a topic or how do I start writing . . . I'm not sure that I can bring those practices to conscious awareness. One thing I always notice with undergraduate writers is that students will write a first draft and it will actually be the last paragraph or the last page where they've figured out what it is that they want to say. I'll say "start with that." It's the reverse in my own writing. I've often found that with a lot of my writing, what I think is the first paragraph actually is, if not the last, one of the closing paragraphs.

CHRISTINE: Any idea why this process happens differently for you as the writing professor?

JOE: I've realized what I need to do is to get into my head where it is I want to go with the piece, and even if I think I'm writing the first paragraph, I look at it and think "no, I've got to say this before I can say that." Then I realize "oh, I've got to say something else," and the paragraph just moves further and further down the page. To some degree, and not deliberately but just through how my mind works, I start with the end, with the insight, with the point that I want to make in the end.

CHRISTINE: Can you tell me a little bit about your writing habits or rituals? You know, time of day or any special place you like to write?

JOE: I don't think I have pronounced rituals. When I'm in the flow of a project, I usually do like to write in the morning, but not at the crack of dawn. I have breakfast and just try to make writing the first thing I do until I run out of steam. I find it difficult to do what I think of as serious writing when other people are in the room. It's not a matter of a particular room, but I want to be in my office at school or my study at home or some sort of quiet place. No matter where I am, I write on a laptop—basically I'm typing when I'm writing.

CHRISTINE: I noticed you were a visiting scholar at Ohio State in the Digital Media and Composition program back in 2010. Has that participation changed your thinking about composing on a computer or how you think about digital technologies in writing for yourself or students?

JOE: Well, first of all, visiting scholar was a nice title that Cindy Selfe cooked up for me, but I wanted to take the seminar, and she said "okay, you will come here as a visiting scholar," and I said "fine."

CHRISTINE: [laughs] No one says no to Cindy!

JOE: That seminar was a wonderful two weeks to think about digital composition. It was a pleasure to really be in the position of being a student and be able to say "I don't know how to do this, show me how" or "I don't get that, can I try again?" I hadn't been in that situation in a long time, and I thought it was a lot of fun. At Duke, for three years in a row I've taught a course on digital writing and how I've taught it has been influenced by that workshop.

CHRISTINE: How so?

JOE: Because all of my writing is now done on a laptop, when I think of my "writing," I'm basically looking into a computer screen. Much of what I read comes to me in digital form, and while I don't have a particular interest in multimedia composing, per se, I just feel that the environment of my work has changed a lot, and I wanted to have some time to think about that. One of the things I've noticed over the past couple of years in my research on student writing is that the advice about how to write online, how to construct and move sentences and paragraphs online, has not yet, I think, made any significant jump from writing on the page. In fact, advice about writing online tends to be divided in much the same way as advice about writing on the page is. The first type of advice tells the writer to be clear and succinct in a kind of Strunk and White way, and that's a lot of advice about never writing more than three-sentence paragraphs and ten-word sentences and so on.

CHRISTINE: [laughs] And the other type?

JOE: On the other hand, there is a new space of, of freedom and release, to be expressive, informal even. From my own writing process, I feel fairly certain that the habits of writers, my own and others, probably are changing as we type on screens rather than scribble on legal pads, and that's something I want to continue to think about. My interest in digital media is less how do you use audio, how do you use video, but what happens to the words when they appear and circulate in different ways.

CHRISTINE: Circulation of work is another topic I have a question about. You've been the editor of the *Cs*, but also you've edited the book series *Studies in Writing and Rhetoric.* Has your work as an editor changed the way you write or made you think about writing differently since you see a wide variety of pieces prior to public circulation?

JOE: I enjoy editing a great deal, and in my mind it's linked to the moment of teaching at the point of revision. You are often working with colleagues to develop and refine their writing projects, so that's just something that seems closely linked to teaching to me that I enjoy very much. Having said that, I thought journal editing and book editing turned out to be more different activities than I had originally thought they would be. If you're working with a twenty- or thirty-page essay with a writer, you can think very closely about how one paragraph turns into the next and even how one sentence turns into another within the paragraph. You can really work with the writing itself. I found as a book editor you work more at a developmental level.

CHRISTINE: Describe what the developmental level means to you.

JOE: At the developmental level I think about chapters, why they're in a particular order, how each leads into the next, and so on, rather than the local level that you can get to in revising an article. Doing both kinds of editing helped me internalize how there really are those two different kinds of advice one can offer a writer. One is the book sort of device which is asking how you develop a project and ask "Does it need to be rethought as a whole?" And then there's another point where you say "Okay, now that you're launched into this project, how do you tweak and refine it?" by which I don't mean superficial copy editing, but instead asking "How do you make the text work at the local level?" When you teach writing and when you try to write, you have to think on both of those levels sometimes and virtually at the same moment. My editing experiences have made me more aware of when I need to shift from one to the other as a writer.

CHRISTINE: What are you working on next?

JOE: The essay I'm working on right now is about a teaching experiment I did where I asked students to deliberately plagiarize a text, to create a text of their own that they assembled entirely through citations of other work. They weren't allowed to use anything original and I think it led to some really interesting work, and basically I just want to share that. That's an easy, a relatively fun, short project. The longer project which I had hoped to finish this summer but got knocked off the agenda with moving is a book which right now I'm calling *Dead Poets and Wonder Boys.* It's about how the teaching of writing has been represented in fiction, movies, and plays. I'm interested in this topic for two reasons. One, writing teachers actually show up a fair amount in contemporary culture. Writing teachers end up playing significant roles in a lot of works.

CHRISTINE: They do!

JOE: I thought that was interesting in and of itself to turn what was a hobby [laughs] and all the movies and books that I had read about academics into research. The second reason I want to do it and what I think gives the project some edge and legitimacy is that even though teachers of writing show up in all these books and movies, very little has been written about these characters, and I don't think we've taken it very seriously. We haven't really thought about what we might want to learn from fictional depictions of the teaching of writing. The little that has been written about representations of writing teachers has been critical in the negative sense, for example we feel *Dead Poet's Society* gets us wrong and existing work explains how it gets us wrong. I think a more interesting question is why are people interested in movies about writing teachers? What do such representations have to tell us as writing teachers about our work? That's the kind of project, because it's a longer one, I turn to in summers. I can write articles and talks during the school year but longer projects need longer blocks of time. I thought this book was going to be done [laughs] more than a summer or two ago. Well, now I feel absolutely sure that by Labor Day 2014 it will be done or I'll just give up! [laughs]

CHRISTINE: Keep it as a hobby, right? [laughs]

JOE: That's right, and that's okay.

3

DÀNIELLE DEVOSS

DÀNIELLE NICOLE DEVOSS is a professor of professional writing at Michigan State University (MSU). She currently serves as associate chair and director of graduate programs in the department of Writing, Rhetoric, and American Cultures. She is the co-author of *Cultures of Copyright* with Martine Rife and co-editor on several projects, including *Because Digital Writing Matters* with Elyse Eidman-Aadahl and Troy Hicks, *Digital Writing Assessment and Evaluation* with Heidi McKee, *Digital Writing Research: Technologies, Methodologies, and Ethical Issues* with Heidi McKee which won the 2007 Computers and Composition Distinguished Book Award. She has also co-edited, with Heidi McKee and Dickie Selfe, *Technological Ecologies and Sustainability*, the first title to be published by Computers and Composition Digital Press, the first digital press in the US with a university press imprint. Her work has appeared in *College English*; *Computers and Composition*; *Kairos: A Journal of Rhetoric, Technology, and Pedagogy*. DeVoss received the Computers and Composition Charles Moran Award for Distinguished Contributions to the field and was recognized as a Beal Outstanding Faculty member at Michigan State in 2016.

In addition to the above accomplishments, DeVoss served for five years as the director of professional writing at Michigan State University, advising all students in the major, serving as internship coordinator, and innovating the curriculum for the undergraduate BA program. She has taught introductory web-authoring courses, upper-level document design classes, and classes focused on nonprofit communications. Beyond the major at MSU, she's also taught courses in digital humanities and in social and cultural entrepreneurship. Her teaching has been informed by and related to other administrative work she's done, including directing the digital humanities initiative and running a creativity, innovation, and entrepreneurship incubator in her college. The interview took place on January 30, 2014, via Skype.

DOI: 10.7330/9781607326625.c003

DÀNIELLE: This is such a fascinating project. I can't tell you how many times I have wanted to talk about this. Just yesterday, a student in a class said, "How do you write? You publish books, right? How do you do this?" And I realized, you know what? For being in a field that tends to privilege pedagogy and process we don't talk about our own very much.

CHRISTINE: One comment that always comes up when your name is mentioned is something like this: "That woman is a machine. She has at least four publications every year, she's always super busy, she collaborates, she does digital, she does print, the whole thing." You've got a really productive CV by the mid-career point. What's your secret?

DÀNIELLE: Golly, wish I knew.

CHRISTINE: [laughs]

DÀNIELLE: I don't say no to anything.

CHRISTINE: Ok, so that's one.

DÀNIELLE: And that is not a good secret. That's a dirty, horrible secret. Honestly, what I think it comes down to is I'm just the type of person, and the type of writer, and I always have been, where I'm more productive the more I have on my plate. Unfortunately, over the last year especially, I've realized that the plate gets full and falls to the ground and smashes.

CHRISTINE: Where do you begin to tackle that plate?

DÀNIELLE: The first thing I do when I get in to work every morning is open up my word processing program and I have a "to-do" list. At the top it has monthly deadlines, and then I have weekly stuff, and then I have daily stuff. So I'll have a list of ten or twelve things that I'm toggling between every day.

CHRISTINE: What does a typical day look like?

DÀNIELLE: Yesterday I had to respond to student projects. I had to finish prepping for class in the afternoon. I had to prep for a committee meeting with a grad student. I had to send out agendas for a couple of different committees that I'm chairing. I had to respond to eight billion emails. I had two letters of recommendation to write, and then in the middle of all that Martine Rife and I are finishing up another book, and I needed to respond to some edits that our editors suggested. So that was like the little research window.

CHRISTINE: Wow.

DÀNIELLE: I have usually fifteen, sixteen apps open on my computer, and I just toggle all day.

CHRISTINE: There is a method to your madness. So, when you come in you don't sit at your desk wondering, "What am I going to work on today?"

DÀNIELLE: No, I don't waste time. And I don't miss deadlines. I have to have a method to manage my writing projects, and I have to have a bunch of writing projects going on at once. I do not manage my time well if I don't have a lot on my plate. That's when I get in trouble.

CHRISTINE: It sounds like you do a lot of writing in your office then. Do you have an end to your workday? When you know you can go home and you are done for the day?

DÀNIELLE: Oh, that's a good question. Well, I don't do any research work at home. I bring student projects home to respond to. I also prep for meetings at home and I prep a lot of teaching stuff at home. I do manuscript reviews at home. I'll do tenure review case reviews at home. Really though, I don't do any of my serious research work at home. The academic writing stays at work. Most days I'm usually here by 7:00 or 7:30, and I try to leave by 5:30. I do not work on Saturdays; I will not work on Saturdays.

CHRISTINE: I can see why you need a day off! [laughs]

DÀNIELLE: [laughs] But I do work Sunday through Friday and it does take this type of schedule to get the amount of writing I get done. If I get to a point on my to-do list where I'm ready for the next couple days, I've met all that day's obligations in terms of correspondence and getting stuff out the door or prepping for classes . . . I guess I leave work when I feel like I won't have a panic attack on the way home!

CHRISTINE: [laughs] That's your day.

DÀNIELLE: But my days are stupid. I don't take breaks, I don't take lunches, I don't chat. I mean it's all work, all the time. I've taken on two administrative positions in the college, and I think that's made me more aware of my time. Now I walk past people chatting in the hallway and I'm always wondering "How do you have time to talk?"

CHRISTINE: Do you feel compelled to write then? You are obviously making time to do it, despite a crazy schedule.

DÀNIELLE: I love to write, unlike a lot of people. I have this problem that I have a big, huge, fat, overblown writer ego!

CHRISTINE: [laughs] How so?

DÀNIELLE: When I write, I think: "Oh, this is BRILLIANT! Oh my gosh; I'm so smart! Oh my gosh, I can link to this person's scholarship, and this article will be great!" So it's really funny because I talk to other writing faculty who don't like writing, who hide their writing, are just terrified of anyone seeing it. I'm the opposite. I'm like, "read this, this is great!" When I have a chance to write it is the best feeling in the world because I have on my computer probably ten or fifteen different folders with outlines for manuscripts I haven't had a chance to get started on that at one point I was like, "Oh my gosh, I have to write this [one manuscript], this is going to be so epic, this is amazing, this needs to be out there! I can pull these students in . . . we'll work on it together and all this is great!"

CHRISTINE: You aren't nervous sharing your drafts?

DÀNIELLE: I'm the opposite. I'm like, "Read this, this is great!" When I have a chance to write it is the best feeling in the world because I have on my computer probably ten or fifteen different folders with outlines for manuscripts I haven't had a chance to get started on. At one point I was like, "Oh my gosh, I have to write this, this is going to be so epic, this is amazing, this needs to be out there, I can pull these students in and we'll work on it together and all this is great!" and the projects just sit there because I don't have the time to do them. When I really have the time to commit to a project and say "Alright I'm going to write this up and get this out the door" . . . oh, it's so wonderful!

CHRISTINE: Yet many faculty just don't have that same motivation or delight in writing. For example, in my own faculty writing group I work with faculty across campus who will always choose prepping for teaching or answering an email over writing. There is something hard about academic writing.

DÀNIELLE: What amazes me is even though so many faculty in our discipline and beyond shy away from writing and recognize how hard it is, the expectations that they set for students are just unbelievable. One time my provost launched this big revisioning project about student success and was getting groups of faculty together for focus groups. My group had twelve faculty from all over the university, and inevitably someone started complaining about the fact that students can't write. And the typical story came out: "Oh well you know they've had that first-year writing, and they can't write." I sat there thinking "You, of all people, have to know how hard writing is" because they write to publish. Finally, I looked at the group and said, "That's so funny. I had an advising session with a student last week who had taken Math 110. She couldn't do Calculus. It was unbelievable." [Christine laughs] And the table just shut down when these faculty realized how ridiculous it was to assume writing should come naturally to students when it is also so difficult for faculty.

CHRISTINE: Is writing more or less difficult for you when you work in a digital space? You have a mix of digital and print projects. Do your composing processes differ?

DÀNIELLE: Even though I publish in print and digital spaces, I think the writing starts in the same place. For me, it always starts in Microsoft Word or in a word processing document. The technological affordances and additions, are affordances and additions, and they come in later. Like, I think, you know I look at our field and there's some people, I suspect digital scholars like Cheryl Ball and Kristen Arola begin composing digitally, and start with media objects, and go from there, but I always start with words on the screen and then take shape. I bet others compose orally.

CHRISTINE: I'm fascinated by faculty who can compose orally. They're driving home, they have a long commute and they call themselves on their faculty voice mail or dictate an oral memo and start a draft from that.

DÀNIELLE: That's so smart and it seems to be a great way to use commute time!

CHRISTINE: I like the idea, but I'm always juggling a latte, and throwing toys in the backseat to entertain kids, and I'm lucky I have a hand on the wheel. I definitely couldn't pick up a phone, and have a brilliant academic thought! [both laugh].

DÀNIELLE: Plus, I like to collaborate, so that would be harder to do unless I was actually talking on the phone with a co-author and recording it.

CHRISTINE: Let's talk about that. You've got a blend of solo and collaborative authorship. How does that work when you collaborate with someone, or a couple of someones?

DÀNIELLE: The solitary authorship thing is a humanities-centric, weird thing. I'm an intellectual bully. [both laugh] Seriously! Martine Rife and I did that *Cultures of Copyright* with Parlor Press, like two years ago, and that started at the C's [Conference for College Composition and Communication] in New Orleans.

CHRISTINE: How so?

DÀNIELLE: John Logie, Martine, and I were doing a panel and at the end of the session we were packing up our stuff, and realized and said "We totally need to do a book on this!" We sat down right there and created the outline for the book and who we wanted to invite and started drafting the proposal.

CHRISTINE: You didn't waste any time! It seems like conferences are space for you to generate new projects.

DÀNIELLE: Jim Purdy and I are working on a book right now, and it was the same sort of weird thing. We were at the Computers and Writing conference, and we were at the end of a session. I said, "We should totally do a book on collaborative, digital, electronic, and physical spaces in writing!" He agreed, and two days later I emailed him saying, "Hey I started drafting the proposal; let's go with this." This also happens with me and Heidi McKee all the time. We are scary because our brains, when it comes to academic productivity, are so similar.

CHRISTINE: How do you collaborate?

DÀNIELLE: When Heidi and I were brainstorming for *Digital Writing Research* on a car ride to Michigan Tech for a conference, we couldn't stop talking because were so excited and then Heidi looks at me, and she's like "Dànielle, Dànielle, Dànielle, we have to be the next Cindy [Selfe] and Gail [Hawisher]!" And I said, "Totally! This is perfect!" And that collection just went from there.

CHRISTINE: How do you feel about collaboration with students?

DÀNIELLE: Some of the really exciting collaborations I've had have actually been with students. There will just be a moment in an undergraduate class, or a graduate seminar, where I will say, "You guys, this idea is fantastic. We need to write this up; we need to do something with this." To make sure we actually do something, what I'll usually do next is send out an email, and say, "Alright, I'm buying us lunch. Who can come and talk about the outline for the manuscript?" and it just goes from there.

CHRISTINE: You probably buy a lot of lunches judging from your CV! [both laugh]

DÀNIELLE: Yes, it's easy to sucker in students, but you know, I feel collaboration is so important to our field. When I came to my position at MSU [Michigan State University], I had this cocky attitude, and I was like "I'm going to do what I like. I'm going to do what I want, and if I get rewarded for it, good, and if I don't get rewarded for it then this isn't a good place for me." So I did a lot of collaborative work deliberately and did work people would call more "servicey-oriented." That's the type of scholarship I value and it worked out pretty well to publish a lot. [laughs]

CHRISTINE: Is there someone in our field whose writing style you like?

DÀNIELLE: I like Johndan Johnson's writing mainly because he drives me crazy. [laughs] I love Anne Wysocki's writing; she also kind of drives me crazy. Both of them have complex arguments but in terms of the writing style and the rhythm of the arguments and the way they like to craft their writing, I find their stuff just absolutely fascinating and motivating. Also Cheryl [Ball] and Kristin [Arola] for sure in part because I feel like we were all at Michigan Tech together for graduate school, and I think they're doing such interesting, exciting stuff they started when they were there.

CHRISTINE: Anyone else?

DÀNIELLE: Oh yes, Kathi Yancey's work. How can you not love the work that she does? It's so beautifully, theoretically infused, but so approachable. That type of writing is so tough to do.

CHRISTINE: Like you, she also puts out a lot of publications. Both of you manage to be very prolific but also avoid the trap of putting out the "garbage pieces" like poorly revised articles, hastily written book chapters, etc. Even though you have a lot of publications, the quality level of your work has been strong and many pieces have won awards. You say you won't miss a deadline, but it also sounds like you don't skip on all the work that goes into the project because you like to write.

DÀNIELLE: Oh, I'm so excited about this book of yours! I want to know how other rhet comp folks write. This is going to be awesome.

4

MELANIE YERGEAU

MELANIE YERGEAU is an assistant professor of English at the University of Michigan. She is the author of *Authoring Autism: On Rhetoric and Neurological Queerness*, and her publications have appeared in venues such as *Kairos, College English, Computers and Composition*, and *Disability Studies Quarterly*, among others. She has served on the board of the Autistic Self Advocacy Network (ASAN), a nonprofit organization run for and by individuals on the autism spectrum, and currently serves on the board of the Autism National Committee.

A rising star in the field of rhetoric and composition, Yergeau has won several awards for her scholarship including the Hugh Burns Outstanding Dissertation Award in Computers and Composition, the *Kairos* Best Webtext Award, and the Computers and Composition Digital Press Accessibility & Digital Composition Award. She has also won several teaching and research awards at Ohio State, her doctoral institution, and University of Michigan. Yergeau's interview took place in her office at University of Michigan on July 8, 2013.

CHRISTINE: For *How Writing Faculty Write*, I'm interviewing productive faculty in the field of writing studies from full professors to new professors. You've just finished your second year of a faculty position at University of Michigan. Have your writing habits changed from graduate school now that you're in your first tenure track appointment?

MELANIE: I've had to adjust to being significantly busier then I was used to being, in part because the teaching load changed from graduate school and adjusting to a new place has taken me a long time. My writing has definitely changed.

CHRISTINE: In what way? The amount you can get done? When you can write?

MELANIE: I feel that my writing has been more like rushed little pockets rather than anything that has evolved over longer periods of time, if that makes sense. I am writing, but my habits have had to adapt to my new environment.

DOI: 10.7330/9781607326625.c004

CHRISTINE: Where do you like to write? Do you write in your office or do you like to go over to the library or a coffee shop?

MELANIE: I rotate. I've mostly been rotating between my office, my house, and a coffee shop, and I'll just go in one location until it stops being productive, and then I'll switch the location. So, I might be here several days a week and then it gets to the point I'm somehow reading about Juno, Alaska, instead of writing . . . [laughs]

CHRISTINE: [laughs] . . . and that's the signal it's time to move to a new writing spot.

MELANIE: Yes, I know I need to try another location. Changing the space where I write does help get me restarted.

CHRISTINE: Though the location may change, do you try to write at the same time of day or follow any other writing rituals?

MELANIE: I'm a morning person so I do try to get it done in the morning.

CHRISTINE: Me too. Before someone interrupts me!

MELANIE: [laughs] I think I just think better in the morning. What happens is if I get something done, it usually happens before 2:00 PM, at which point, I'm fried. I think the only exception to writing later is if I have a looming deadline.

CHRISTINE: Deadlines are a great motivator.

MELANIE: And stressful. Often what will happen is I'm stressed out the entire day and I'm not getting any writing done because I'm worried. When 9:00 PM hits suddenly I'm writing, and I'm up until 6:00 AM finishing it. [laughs]

CHRISTINE: Sounds like you haven't moved that far away from the all-night writing from graduate school.

MELANIE: At those times no, but they are pretty infrequent.

CHRISTINE: Your doctoral institution Ohio State and University of Michigan are both R1s. Were you surprised at the publication requirements, or did you know what you were getting into in terms of how much writing you need to do?

MELANIE: I don't think I was surprised. Things were made pretty clear coming in, and there are a lot of similarities between the institutions. The biggest difference in writing expectation I've had to deal with is the place of digital writing at my new institution.

CHRISTINE: Can you tell me a little about the difference?

MELANIE: I initially came in wanting to do a digital book, and the advice I've gotten from pretty much everybody across the board in my department is do not do that.

CHRISTINE: Did they say why?

MELANIE: The feeling I've got is that the department would be supportive, but they have reservations about the college when it comes time for tenure. I've had to switch things out and adjust—my book project has nothing to do with my dissertation.

CHRISTINE: You won an award for your digitally born dissertation at a Computers and Writing Conference and you did one of the first digital dissertations at Ohio State. So, what's your new project going to be since you have to think in a print mindset for your first book project?

MELANIE: My new project is exclusively about autism and rhetoric. One of my dissertation chapters had to do with autism, so in some ways I think the spirit of that chapter is what's carrying the new book project.

CHRISTINE: How is the writing going?

MELANIE: I've really had to think differently. I'm used to writing digitally, especially with the longer projects.

CHRISTINE: Can you explain your digital composing process?

MELANIE: One of the things I liked about the dissertation was that if I couldn't think in words I could create a video clip and then suddenly I was thinking back in words, again and could be typing and writing. Making a digital text lets me section things out differently. When I wrote the dissertation, I was writing in smaller web-based segments, because when you're writing for the web, you aren't writing thirty pages at a time.

CHRISTINE: It sounds like print may be more difficult because of the linear nature, but also because of the scope?

MELANIE: I think that's been one of the challenges about now switching back to print. I'm writing in these little bursts, but a print book has to be something that's more long-form. Finding ways to thread those patches together has been really difficult and interesting. I'm in the midst of doing that right now. I'm actually working furiously to get a chapter draft down because several people from my department are going to workshop it with me in mid-August.

CHRISTINE: And this would be the first chapter of this book project, or are you further along than that? Are you on a second or a third?

MELANIE: The one I'm working on is a second chapter, or at least what I think is going to be a second chapter. The first chapter is fairly short and tone setting, but this one, I think, is the first really meaty chapter.

CHRISTINE: You mentioned that faculty in the department will workshop it with you. Is this a set faculty writing group in your department or something broader across the institution for new faculty?

MELANIE: Workshopping drafts has developed as a mentoring thing in my department. I think it was early last year the junior faculty met together with the department chair and associate chair, and we just talked about some of the things that would be helpful for us to publish, and one of the things that came up was just workshopping stuff, even crap.

CHRISTINE: Crap? [laughs]

MELANIE: At least for me, that's what it was. I'm the type of writer that needs people to look at my crap before I can go and make it beautiful or whatever else that makes sense. Of course though, it's sort of challenging because even though I think that the group of people who'd be workshopping it are fine in seeing my crap, [laughs] I'm really apprehensive in showing it to them.

CHRISTINE: Who is workshopping the draft? Other new faculty in the same boat working on first tenure books?

MELANIE: No, actually. The people who are workshopping it, at least this time around, are all tenured. That's also what kind of makes me really nervous.

CHRISTINE: How so?

MELANIE: I don't know. Individually, the people who are part of that group have been really helpful in the past. I have an essay coming out in *Disability Studies Quarterly* and Anne Curzan was really instrumental in helping me publish that essay.

CHRISTINE: Is the challenge the idea of working with the bigger project of a book?

MELANIE: I think for me I need a lot of time, which is why this summer has been good. Like, my head is just in book space and that's one of the problems, I think, about the school year structure. It's hard to maintain that momentum, so I know I need the workshop feedback to help me revise and continue writing.

CHRISTINE: Do you have any tricks to managing how you develop a larger (and new) writing project?

MELANIE: In some ways I think the dissertation digital writing stuff has served me well for this new project. It's helped me to scaffold a bit better and map things out, so even though I still am writing in bits and pieces, which is in some ways problematic, it actually works from an outlining perspective.

CHRISTINE: Where does the digital writing experience translate to writing for print specifically?

MELANIE: I'm creating concept maps and using Scrivener. I don't know if you've ever used that program, but . . .

CHRISTINE: I've heard of it, but I've never used it.

MELANIE: . . . It's really useful because it allows you to create hierarchies of pages, and you can look at a document in different views. For example, there's a cork board view where you can organize ideas with little notecard looking things or you can go into more of a word processing view. That's helpful for me because each different perspective enables me to see connections among things and where I might be able to patch things together.

CHRISTINE: I'm thinking in terms of writing; it might make writing actually a little bit stronger cause you're less married to where ideas

belong. Do you find that when you look at the overall conceptual map, something you thought belonged in chapter 2, would be amazing in the introduction in chapter 3 and you don't care so much about moving it? [laughs]

MELANIE: Absolutely, because it's all drag and drop, so if you have three little paragraphs in one document you can put in a sidebar and can move them. Plus, when you want to compile all of the notecards or sections, you just compile it and Scrivener will export it to Word or Adobe. That program somewhat eases the transition for me when thinking of giant web text to a print book. I think that I'm really associational as a thinker. Sometimes is just seems like I have forty different ideas and I have no idea how to arrange them or make them make any sense.

CHRISTINE: You work with the intersection of autism and rhetoric studies. How do form and content work together for you?

MELANIE: In some ways the narrative aspect has replaced the digital aspect for me in the book project. In order for me to write I have to have a personal investment of some kind in the topic.

CHRISTINE: Does this investment help you commit to writing each day?

MELANIE: Definitely. With this project, there's certainly that affective dimension to it, having been in this community for years and having this disability myself. I react to all the stuff that gets propagated in the mass media, the ways in which autistic people are treated or not treated or segregated from their peers. Narrative as a methodology is really important to the project that I'm currently working on, because there are just so many false stories circulating out there and I can write back.

CHRISTINE: Is writing cathartic for you?

MELANIE: Sometimes I get frozen writing when I'm reading really awful stuff for research. Right now I'm reading pharmacological studies on autism and, like, looking at research studies that pump autistic teens full of anti-depressants to make them stop having sexual feelings—chemical castrations, essentially.

CHRISTINE: I can imagine it is difficult to write about what you are reading when you have your own perspective as an autistic person.

MELANIE: I know I need to write something about it because it is important for my research, but right now I just want to set it on fire.

CHRISTINE: It must be difficult to have this disturbing information in your head while you're writing and to also have to think of a way to manage to write about it.

MELANIE: I think that's kind of the writer's block I've encountered recently. I rarely have writer's block on other subjects, particularly when I write digitally. Doing the digital dissertation is what enabled me to get it done, to be honest, because if I was at a place where I couldn't write, I could design. So, I could take photographs, and this was part of dissertating.

CHRISTINE: Do you ever have a day where you say "I want to write something that is completely not about autism; I just want to write something totally new."

MELANIE: Every day. [laughs] When I started at OSU [Ohio State University], I was not doing disabilities studies. I went to OSU because it was an interest. I had very much a personal interest in it, but I went because I was interested in rhetorical history and feminist rhetoric. I was interested in the ways in which women preachers at the turn of the twentieth century used media. It was very far afield.

CHRISTINE: That's *very* far afield from your new book project. [laughs]

MELANIE: [laughs] Sometimes I wonder why'd I stop doing that? But in my second quarter at OSU, I took the disability studies class with Brenda Brueggemann, and I realized there is a certain exigency to studying disabilities that I didn't feel with what I entered there to do. Still, the day I get really sick of autism, I can sort of pick up the stuff I started doing my first year of the PhD program!

CHRISTINE: That is the nice aspect to our field of writing studies—you can always shift gears and find a new topic.

MELANIE: I've also realized that there are endless ways to approach the topic of autism too, which offers a lot of choices if I get bored with one specific angle. I think that there's also this sense of community around disability studies issues, more broad than the autism and stuff, like actually knowing the people who are doing the work, who are invested in it, and also realizing that the research and writing I do potentially has tangible and material impacts on people.

CHRISTINE: It does. So you approach writing realizing that it's not just about writing the academic book that sells two hundred copies and mostly to libraries.

MELANIE: No, it is definitely a political project.

CHRISTINE: Since you are part of this writing community, is there somebody within the field whose style of writing you admire?

MELANIE: I think there are a lot of people I admire. One would be Margaret Price. What I think I like about her writing is that it has that sort of narrative dimension to it. She's a poet, and you can just tell the way that she writes she is. There's a certain, like, art to her work, but it's also serious and scholarly. I admire Brenda Brueggemann or Paul Hallacher. Paul is an essayist, and his stuff is so easy to read, but at the same time it's incredibly challenging and rigorous. I get so much out of reading stuff that has those different layers to it.

CHRISTINE: Is there, you know, somebody you know who is an up and coming scholar who is doing novel things with writing?

MELANIE: My answer's mixed because not all of them are academic. A lot of them are autistic bloggers and disability bloggers. One is Elizabeth Anderson Gray, and she's an assistant professor at National Louis University. Her field is outside of ours because she's in special education but she's an autistic blogger, and I just love the style of her blog. Her writing reminds me a lot of Brenda Brueggemann in a lot of ways . . .

CHRISTINE: How so?

MELANIE: The writing seems like it's stream of consciousness, but it's not. It's very deliberate. Stephanie Kerschbaum, who is also in our field, posted the link to her blog and said "This reminds me of Gertrude Stein," and I thought "Yes!" It's hard to explain but it's just a really beautiful style. Another writer I admire is Julia Bascom, and she is not an academic. She works for the autistic self-advocacy network and just edited an autistic disability rights anthology called *Loud Hands*, and so she has a very essayistic writing style, but it's also really clearly activist, engaging with really dense theoretical concepts.

CHRISTINE: This is interesting because it sounds like scholarly work that maintains a direct political advocacy.

MELANIE: Bascom blends politics and theory so beautifully. She, like many of the other writers I admire, claims autism is a culture. In many of the writers I admire there are ideas about autistic style or autistic rhetorics and the writers argue for reclaiming things that are traditionally cast as symptoms into aspects of a disability culture.

CHRISTINE: Since you have found your subject area, and you are known for doing disability studies as a scholar, what, what are you going to do for your next project? What's the next book or article you'd like to do?

MELANIE: I'd like to come back to some of the things from my dissertation and look at disability studies more generally within the field of composition. What I'm doing is like really specifically focused on one particular disability slash Kairotic moment, but I'd like to come back again to looking at access and ways of moving through the field thinking about disability as a critical modality.

CHRISTINE: As a new writing professor, you have a lot of time to write about these issues. Is there something that keeps you motivated to keep writing every day?

MELANIE: Yes, absolutely. Because I know I am writing work that may change people's perceptions about autism or disabilities I feel a responsibility to keep arguing for a change in ideas with the field of writing studies about how people with disabilities write. Beyond that, I find putting together a project that matters to me, and hopefully to others, extremely satisfying.

5

JESSICA ENOCH

JESSICA ENOCH is the associate professor and Director of Academic Writing at the University of Maryland, where she teaches classes in rhetorical education, feminist rhetorics, rhetorical historiographies of gender, and public memory. She is author of *Refiguring Rhetorical Education: Women Teaching African American, Native American, and Chicano/a Students, 1865–1911* and co-editor of *Burke in the Archives: Using the Past to Transform the Future of Burkean Studies.* Her work has been recognized through awards such as Kathleen Ethel Welch Outstanding Article Award, Theresa J. Enos Award for Best Essay in *Rhetoric Review,* and the James Berlin Memorial Outstanding Dissertation Award. She is currently at work on a book manuscript titled *Domestic Occupations: Spatial Rhetorics and Women's Work 1830–1950* that explores how spatial rhetorics inform women's work opportunities, as well as a bilingual anthology of Mexican newspaper women (with Cristina Ramírez).

Enoch has worked at several locations during her career including University of New Hampshire and University of Pittsburg prior to coming to the University of Maryland and has taught historical surveys of women's rhetoric, technical writing, and creative non-fiction, in addition to first year writing. Enoch's interview took place on August 15, 2013, via Skype.

CHRISTINE: You've been out in the field for ten years and you've been really, really productive. You've got books, you've got an edited collection, articles, and overall a very consistent, even amazing productivity.

JESSICA: Thank you.

CHRISTINE: How are you able to get regular output, but also very high quality at the same time?

JESSICA: I think, to be honest, one of the things that I know has helped me so much throughout my career is that I was a college athlete and so I had to manage my time. I really had to learn how to manage my time very well as an undergraduate and the scholastics and academics were really underscored in my field hockey team. We were a very

DOI: 10.7330/9781607326625.c005

competitive field hockey team so from eighteen on I have focused so much on understanding what are the most important things to get done and how do I get those types of things done. I'm sure I'll be mentioning this person a lot through my interview but Cheryl Glenn was my mentor and my dissertation advisor and she has an amazing work ethic and also has a really nice personal life. I really watched her in graduate school seeing how she would get things out and how she would plan her projects. I was her research assistant for four years so I really got to watch how she got writing done and got projects done really well.

CHRISTINE: Well and how to put a project together it sounds like too. Because part of time management is figuring out what's essential at this moment in a project.

JESSICA: Exactly. Being a research assistant helped me see a model of how she did it . . . what books did she check out, how expansive was her project, how did she move along with her chapters, how was she balancing that book with all the other work that she did, and so on. I studied her while I was in graduate school just as much as I studied rhetoric and composition, as in how can I do what she's doing and balance a personal life.

CHRISTINE: And not be a twenty-four-hour workaholic.

JESSICA: I really admired how she balanced her life. You've mentioned how to make work high quality, and she modeled that as well. Cheryl would have other people read [her work], and now one thing I try to do before I send anything out to a journal is I send it out to who I think that they would send my essay to for a review. Before even submitting I can do a revise and resubmit session with a scholar in our field who *CCC* or *College English* might send a manuscript to.

CHRISTINE: That's a great suggestion for people that would read this collection, and another way learning from a publishing role model can help.

JESSICA: I think that a lot of people see sending an essay to a journal as being like a draft and see what people think, but I think that I've had pretty good success with essays by really spending a lot of time getting them into pretty good shape before they go in. They still get better through my work with editors, but they've already kind of gone through two editorial revision processes with the journal because I'll send a draft of an essay to David Gold because I know they could possibly send it to him. Of course he would not say that he would read it again if they did that but I'm just saying I imagine who the reader would be before actually submitting.

CHRISTINE: So you probably have a better sense, you would say, of your audience prior to sending it out for publication? It's not just that you're writing for the *CCC* but you're writing for maybe a specific person in your field? You have somebody kind of in your mind that's going to be interested in your article?

JESSICA: Right. That's one thing that I just really love about our field is that it's small enough that you really can kind of think, I wonder what David [Gold] would think of this, or what would Cheryl [Glenn] think of this, or Gesa Kirsch. Jack Selzer told me in graduate school to imagine your essays like a conversation. You know you're not competing against someone but just try to add to the conversation. I think that takes a lot of the pressure off in terms of saying that every essay has to be this groundbreaking text. Instead how can you just contribute in a smart way to a conversation you're really interested in? And I think that's one of the reasons why I am consistently working on something because there are just a lot of conversations that really excite me in the field. I've recently been doing some publishing on digital humanities and I would not say that I'm an expert in digital stuff but I just think it's a fascinating thing to think about how digital archives and digital platforms are going to change the historiography. So it's been fun to just be an amateur and just get to know the subject and try to publish on it but not to claim that now I'm going to start building databases or anything like that.

CHRISTINE: Rhetoric and composition is more flexible than other fields but you do seem to provide a good example of somebody who is open to exploration.

JESSICA: Right. I wouldn't suggest for a graduate student at this point to just dip her foot into the digital humanities and write an essay about it, but for me at this point I feel like I have pretty good sense of how our historiography works in our field, and I know that people in the digital humanities are talking about that. And so I have a rich set of questions and background in our field from my past projects that I can use to interface with that new field. I understand why I'm interested in the digital humanities, but I don't feel like that has to be something now that I'm going to write my new book on. Still, I've got three or four side projects developing with this digital interest that just kind of keep popping up and I say, "Oh, I guess I'm going to write another essay on this!" [laughs]

CHRISTINE: How do you tend to juggle multiple projects? Some writing faculty are laser focused and say just working on chapter 1 of a book, but then others have like three or four things going on at one time. How do you juggle several items, or do you? Maybe you don't.

JESSICA: No, I do. And sometimes . . . I think that there's like a saturation point where there are too many balls in the air and things just stop getting done. That has happened to me before where I say, "Okay, from here on out I can't work on four different things at the same time." But, I have learned that I can and I really like to have my major projects, such as the third chapter of my book manuscript, and I have these other side projects, many of which involve collaboration.

CHRISTINE: Does collaboration help you actively managing working on several writing projects?

JESSICA: Yes, in fact I just was writing with one of my collaborators today. I love to send our finished draft to her on a Friday and then kind of take the weekend and then it's doing whatever it does at her house.

CHRISTINE: It's getting worked on even when you aren't the one writing it. It sounds like this is a deliberate time management strategy.

JESSICA: The same thing happens with my day. I really try to start my day around four-thirty or so with my book manuscript and then after the kids wake up and eat breakfast I work on the collaborative piece in the early morning. Now I'm running the writing program here at Maryland so then in the afternoon I do writing program stuff. I break my day up so that I'm always kind of working on the book but then working on these other things in the *second tier* of my day. I'm like, I think I'm most sharp in the morning, in the early morning, so I try to do the book stuff because if I put that aside then the book won't get done. But I've been doing some [editorial work] . . . and I usually work on that in the midmorning to afternoon and David Gold and I just finished a special issue in *College English* on the digital humanities and rhetorical historiography, so if I can find a place in my day then I will add another project. If I'm finding that I can't rotate it in then that's when I realize there's just too much on my plate.

CHRISTINE: I direct the writing program too and know how that goes. If you don't do your writing the first thing in the day, some WPA crisis will sneak up on you.

JESSICA: It's so true.

CHRISTINE: There were several people in the collection I've asked about managing writing program administration and scholarly work. Some of the interviewees just try to integrate the two where they write about what it is that they're administering, but it sounds like in your case these areas of your writing faculty life are separate.

JESSICA: Well, I've only been doing this since July 1st so who knows what's going to happen? [laughs] Jordynn Jack and I are doing an edited collection so I honestly could not turn my WPA work into scholarly stuff because there's no more time in my day to write about it, but you know maybe once one project goes I can find something really interesting to do. The writing program is doing assessment this year and I could see possibly thinking about that but that would be a ball in the air that I could not do writing wise.

CHRISTINE: No time.

JESSICA: I see myself as a slow writer because I feel like I write very slowly. If someone told me to write a ten-page paper by tomorrow, I would not be able to do that. I write very slowly but I write every day. And I think of Don Murray when I was at the University of New Hampshire, we went out to lunch and he said write a word a day, a sentence a day, just try to sit at your desk and write a little bit each day and that's really what works best for me . . . I could never write a lot at once.

CHRISTINE: And with every writing project added, each one requires a slow writing process?

JESSICA: Yes. I think of myself as a really slow writer because when I go to the 4Cs [Conference for College Composition and Communication] conference my paper has been done three days before I get on the plane because I'm always terrified of having to write on the plane. I mean, I would just not go to my panel.

CHRISTINE: [laughs] And you always see those people on the plane.

JESSICA: Right. And I usually admire those people because I think, "Wow, you must have such confidence in yourself" because I would be bouncing like a ball in the plane aisle with panic. And if you have children you know you just can't count on all of a sudden being able to write. You might not get that day before the conference to write the paper so . . .

CHRISTINE: Definitely not. Sick kid, snow day . . .

JESSICA: Right. You have to work time sensitive writing in whenever you can because you might not have the time you expect.

CHRISTINE: There are a couple of books out about academic motherhood and balancing. I don't know if you've read any of them but they take opposite positions on how mothers can function as academics. Some of them say scholarship can be done and you can balance a prolific career and motherhood, and others acknowledge you won't always do both well. You won't make all your kids' events and you're not going to get all those articles written. Others argue you can do both but you have to be really, really good at time management, which I think is what you're trying to say here.

JESSICA: I guess so. To be honest, it was funny because I have three children and I saw an article the other day that was like the best number to have is four, don't have . . . either have two or four, never have three and I just shut it. Because I was like, I don't want to know why I shouldn't have three because we're not having any more.

CHRISTINE: You don't need it in your head.

JESSICA: We can't get rid of one because of what a book says. [laughs] I'm very interested in parental leave and helping junior faculty members have children. Trying to talk to junior faculty members about having kids and being on the tenure line and publishing. I often don't read those books because they might introduce an issue that I haven't yet encountered and I feel like I'm up to my eyes with it already.

CHRISTINE: Well yes, when you're living it it's different than reading about it when you had to handle it fifteen years ago or something.

JESSICA: Right. The part of it that I think is critical is rather than evaluating if you're being a good mom or not is to help others. How do you get the leave you need? That structural piece is what kills you because if you don't get the leave that you deserve or that the university provided because your department chair isn't familiar with the policy or you don't know how to talk about leave, that's what is going to bring you down both ways, family wise and scholarly wise. I think a lot of my scholarship has been autobiographical in ways, like when I was pregnant with my son and I was very nervous about what should we do for childcare. I wrote an essay on childcare centers during World War II. You'll notice if someone could follow my career look at "Oh she's writing about this, so she must be having this issue!" [laughs]

CHRISTINE: It's an interesting way to work out the balance between motherhood and scholarship. I have to admit, when I read the books on balancing writing with mothering, I did wonder "Why am I reading this? I could be reading *Family Circle* and figuring out cool things to put in my kids' lunches." [laughs]

JESSICA: [laughs] Right. When a book says you can't publish a lot and be a mother and you're already doing it, just put it down.

CHRISTINE: Let's talk about another part of writing faculty identity. Your work seems to bridge both the rhetoric and composition sides of our field. Do you identify more on the rhetoric side of the house or composition side?

JESSICA: That is interesting. I don't know. When I talk to people they see me as a feminist rhetorician and historiographer. Yet I very much see myself as someone who is rhetoric and comp. I have often taught the intro to comp theory course, the pedagogy course for new instructors, so that even though it doesn't come out as much in my scholarship. I've published a little bit on teaching, and I'm working on an article right now that focuses on teaching digital archives with undergraduates, so I guess I would see myself as both. I think where you are makes you think of yourself as more one way or another. Here at Maryland it's very rhetorical, so you're kind of part of the group of "the rhetoric people" among the faculty. Whatever you're working on and wherever you are, you sort of dip one way or dip another. As WPA I better be someone who's good with composition because we're making decisions about assessment, about the syllabi. I wouldn't want to be someone who's just doing rhetorical theory without applications to the classroom. For me rhetoric and composition are so close even when I'm trying to make this distinction I'm asking, "What is rhetoric, what is composition without rhetoric" . . . does that makes sense to you?

CHRISTINE: It does. But there are writing faculty that identify more with the RSA [Rhetoric Society of America] and they would never go the 4Cs and vice versa.

JESSICA: There have been moments where I like detaching myself from the classroom and just being able to write about women's rhetorical history. When I wrote an essay on sterilization it was kind of liberating in a way to think, I don't need to come back to the classroom and talk about what this application might be. But then also writing these essays about teaching it's engaging to me to ask, "How do my ideas about rhetorical history translate into kind of thinking about teaching writing? How do those two things go together?" I see myself as both rhetoric and composition, and I think that's a mentoring thing too. My mentors in graduate school went to both 4Cs and RSA. I grew up professionally thinking like you don't have to make that decision.

CHRISTINE: **How are you mentoring your own students? Are you teaching them scholarship habits your mentors taught you? Or is your writing life sort of separate from your teaching life?**

JESSICA: There are some things that you couldn't tell a graduate student, such as "You know, I think you should be writing this draft, or at this point it should take you this amount of time, or do freewriting first and then come talk to me." But I think that there are some critical things about academic genres that are so helpful from a mentoring point of view to teach students, especially with writing projects like grant proposals. How do you identify what a definition section is as opposed to a significance section and what are kind of key terms and key verbs that you use? Those are things I think of as pulling back the veil a little bit, which is what Cheryl [Glenn] did for me. I'm also very calendar based, so I sit down with my students and we say, "Okay, you'll have your draft to me by this time and then I'll get to back to you and then you'll have your next draft to me by this time." However they get to that first draft is fine but the biggest thing I think I do helpfully, I hope, is to teach graduate students how to revise from comments. If you're talking to a graduate student and she says something like, "But this paragraph took me ten hours to write!" and they just want to keep it even though you're trying to tell them it doesn't make any sense . . . or . . . [laughs]

CHRISTINE: **Or you've lost focus or something like that . . .**

JESSICA: Right. You're moving into a different topic and it's not working. I try to teach them that . . . you have to just be willing to throw your writing away. I think you can teach people about revision and how to recognize when is it starting to work, when are you hitting a stride and now it's making sense. I would shudder to have you talk to any of the graduate students I work with, how many drafts they go through with their dissertation chapters and things like that, but that's the kind of feedback I got and I think it's also that quality issue you're talking about before. After having Cheryl read draft after draft after draft, there were moments I remember thinking "I'm getting there. I finally understand what she means." I understood the writing was starting to be engaging and . . . provocative in a way rather than planned. I think I'm pretty rigorous with my students in the same way.

CHRISTINE: **You are able to teach from your own experience with writing.**

JESSICA: And I'm now okay with Anne Lamott's shitty first drafts! [laughs] I think that that's part of the writing process. I use writing pedagogy from my 101 class with myself all the time. I mean, I talk about myself as a writer with my students constantly. I think talking with people about how I revise and what revision means has helped me become a much better writer because of how I teach writing. Rather than saying, like, I teach writing one way and then do it a different way, I teach topic sentences the way I write topic sentences. I mean I love topic sentences. [laughs]

CHRISTINE: Who doesn't? They're fabulous.

JESSICA: Right. Who doesn't love a great topic sentence? But you could ask people in my first-year writing class and the graduate student who just walked outside my office that that's something that I will write as a comment on work. Like this topic sentence isn't working, your last one . . . this is a great topic sentence, it's really transitioning well. And if you can hit a topic sentence, you're in good shape in my mind.

CHRISTINE: Let's jump from the smaller scope of a topic sentence to something large, like your book. You are working on your second solo-authored book. You've gone through a book writing process once already. What's different about the process this time around versus your tenure book or first book process?

JESSICA: I think there are things about it that I'm smarter about in terms of archival research and knowing when I've gotten enough and I can start writing and things along those lines. But I still . . . there's still a ton of anxiety around this book, you know. I want it to be done. I don't think this is my book . . . this isn't like the life story of Jess Enoch. I have another book that I would like to write and I would like this one to be done so I can move on to the next one. I want to write something that's really interesting and is going to . . . be impactful in some sort of way, right? At the same time, I still wonder, is this chapter good enough? The anxiety is more about quality of chapters than anxiety over writing a book.

CHRISTINE: I see.

JESSICA: I think the difference is knowing that I can do it but wanting to move a little bit faster but still wanting the quality to be really good. In this new book I'm having to learn a lot about architecture and spatial theory and sometimes I'm like, I could have written something that was . . . [laughs] a little bit less ambitious in terms of what I needed to know.

CHRISTINE: Do you have a working title for this book, [laughs] if I throw it in brackets in the transcription?

JESSICA: *Claiming Space: Feminist Rhetorical Investigations of Educational Geographies.* I don't know how to have a good title that is not a mouthful, but at least the front part isn't so bad.

CHRISTINE: Well and hey, you've got those keywords in there.

JESSICA: Yeah!

CHRISTINE: Good for a database search.

JESSICA: It's been really fun. I love it. I mean I love working on it and it's kind of been like a safe thing. I'm working on this book that I really like and I love being able to go to these places and do this archival work, but now I'm pushing towards, I hope, the final quarter and asking "What am I going to do?" [laughs]

CHRISTINE: [laughs] The next project is always right around the corner for the busiest writers I'm finding.

JESSICA: I think one of the things that's been a problem for me is that I'm so interested in historiography and I know my next project, like on public memory and historiography, that I'm starting to work on it. But I've got to finish the space book. I've got one part of my brain thinking about this third book and presenting on this at conferences and thinking the space book is done, but it's not. I'm in the middle of my third major chapter. I need to compose that. I need to go back to the second chapter. So I've got a lot to do, but I'm hoping. I'm giving myself a year and a half and that's my deadline. It's got to be done. So . . . it will be! [laughs]

CHRISTINE: [laughs] Yes, it will.

JESSICA: It was fun to talk about writing today. It's funny, but as professors we don't talk about writing as much as we do as graduate students so I'm glad you are doing this project. I hit a gold mine in graduate school by working with Jack Selzer and Cheryl to learn how to write but I know not everyone has that opportunity.

6

JONATHAN ALEXANDER

JONATHAN ALEXANDER is chancellor's professor of English at the University of California, Irvine, where he also serves as the campus writing coordinator and director of the Center for Excellence in Writing & Communication. He is the author, editor, or co-author of eleven books, has guest edited nine special issues of journals, authored or co-authored over fifty articles, and is general editor of *College Composition and Communication.* Alexander's notable publications include *Techne: Queer Meditations on Writing the Self,* co-authored with Jacqueline Rhodes, Computers and Composition Digital Press, which won the 2016 Lavender Rhetorics Award, and *On Multimodality: New Media in Composition Studies,* which won the 2015 CCCC Outstanding Book Award and the 2014 Computers & Composition Distinguished Book Award. He is also a three-time recipient of the Ellen Nold Award for Best Articles in the field of Computers and Composition Studies.

Originally a scholar of comparative literature, Alexander became interested in composition as a field during his first position at a regional Colorado State University campus in Pueblo. After teaching in a computer lab for the first time, Alexander's early writing studies research focused on using computers to teach writing and later focused on intersections between sexuality, technologies, and writing. His interview took place July 23, 2013, via Skype.

CHRISTINE: You've argued with Jaclyn Rhodes in "Queer: An Impossible Subject for Composition" that the relationship, the intersections between rhetoric and writing and queer studies are relatively sparse and under read. How are you working to make these connections more explicit in rhet-comp projects such as *Understanding Rhetoric* guide for first-year writers or the *On Multimodality* text about to come out?

JONATHAN: That's a great question, and one that I think about a lot because I know that if one were just to look at my list of publications, I could certainly be accused of being all over the map. It looks like

DOI: 10.7330/9781607326625.c006

I pull from and contribute to a lot of different strains and conversations that occur broadly in English studies, in the humanities, and within comp-rhet. From inside, [laughs] I actually feel like I'm writing about the same thing over and over and over again, just with a different emphasis.

CHRISTINE: How so?

JONATHAN: You mentioned the *Understanding Rhetoric* text. That is not a text that is explicitly about sexuality or that is explicitly grappling with issues of sexual discourses or sexual literacies as I call them, and yet, that text, in my mind, was absolutely informed by my work in sexuality studies and in thinking of sexuality studies through writing studies. For example, my co-authors and I have an entire chapter just on identity, the importance of thinking about a writer's identity and the performance of identity, and how writers can adopt and take on different identities in order to generate different kinds of knowledge. We use as an example Barbara Ehrenreich, *Nickel and Dimed,* where she becomes a menial laborer, so that she can learn, in an embodied way, what it means to be in the working class in the country.

CHRISTINE: It's a very specific example that students can understand.

JONATHAN: It's not explicitly about sexuality. The notion that we can learn through the body, learn by taking on other roles, by playing with identity seems to me something that I very much take with me from my studies in sexuality and informs my understanding of performativity. In my research, my appreciation for how an identity shapes what one can know and the insights that one can generate from that perspective. Does that make sense?

CHRISTINE: It does. Now that you mention this as your guiding principle when writing, I can see there is clearly a deliberate way of approaching them. Even if this overall thread remains the same, how does it play out when you compose in different mediums, such as print or graphics or digital spaces? Does your writing process differ depending on the end medium?

JONATHAN: [laughs] Yes. Absolutely. I am probably pretty traditional as an academic, in terms of thinking about what I want that end product to be. Maybe I actually shouldn't say that. I don't know if it's traditional or not. Probably your project will tell me. [laughs]

CHRISTINE: I guess we'll see. [laughs]

JONATHAN: It seems very useful to just think rhetorically. To whom do I want to talk and how do I want to talk to them? And so, I think very much in terms of specific journals, the readerships of those journals, book series, the readerships of those book series, and think, "Okay, I want to talk about these issues to these people. What is the genre medium that will most effectively reach out to that readership?" I also want to push what we know collectively as readers within that field. I don't really publish in any journal that I don't also consider myself a reader of, so I consider myself part of the readership of that journal. So knowing what I know about that readership, how can I try to advance a particular conversation or at least contribute to it? But then also in terms of choice of, of medium, I consider what works to forward the aim of the discussion.

CHRISTINE: Can you describe how this happened in a specific piece?

JONATHAN: When Jackie and I did the piece for *Enculturation* on queer archives ["Queer Rhetoric and the Pleasure of the Archive"], we had originally conceived that piece as a print publication, and we targeted a journal. We drafted that piece with that journal in mind, forgetting that we had actually presented that material at a presentation with multimedia. We realized this as we were writing the print piece and that that was a bad thing to forget. [laughs]

CHRISTINE: [laughs]

JONATHAN: It clearly wasn't going to work as a print piece. [laughs]

CHRISTINE: Not with the multimedia element.

JONATHAN: We had to go back to the multimedia that was originally used in the presentation, and I thought, "This will work better just as a multimedia piece," and then all of a sudden the multimedia journals, the multimediated journals like *Kairos* and *Enculturation,* became the ones that we were thinking of. But coming to this discovery of the right audience, the right journal, and the right media is definitely a process.

CHRISTINE: Having both print and digital options seems to open up the types of questions writing faculty have to ask before and during a writing project.

JONATHAN: On one hand thinking about what audience you are trying to reach, what readership you want to try to tap into, but then also trying to be true to the source material as well is a balance. The *Enculturation* piece was a good lesson for us. In the *On Multimodality* book, we faced the exact same issue and the Studies in Writing and Rhetoric editor, Victor Villanueva really fought with us over the last year about whether this would be better as a print book or as a multimedia book.

CHRISTINE: What was the debate?

JONATHAN: In our profession we actually have options. There's the Computers in Composition Digital Press, there's the Sweetland Digital Press, but Jackie and I decided that what we'd ultimately do was go with a print book because our concerns and our critique in the book, they're pitched more to the profession as a whole.

CHRISTINE: Rather than a *Computers in Composition* type community?

JONATHAN: Precisely. Our feeling was that we wanted to talk to the larger composition studies community about the general uptake of new media tools in the composition classroom as opposed to furthering the conversation within a much smaller community. I feel the products of those digital presses are still primarily read by people in *Computers in Composition.* I hope that will change.

CHRISTINE: Returning to your suggestion about thinking rhetorically, it seems that you put audience as your first concern for this book.

JONATHAN: That was very much a choice of readership; about thinking about to whom were we really talking to and what did we want to say about the material that we're working with. Victor did, I think rightly, insist that we have a disclaimer in the introduction that says, you're going to get a lot more out of this book if you read it with your computer. [laughs]

CHRISTINE: [laughs]

JONATHAN: I think for *On Multimodality* that that was the right instinct, but those are complicated questions for any writer of rhetoric scholarship. I've been thinking about them.

CHRISTINE: It does seem to be a chicken and egg scenario for writers who are looking to write about multimodal issues. First, you've got to get the people to build the articles and the web text and that sort of thing and then the hope is the readership will come as a result, but how does the readership expand beyond the scholars already comfortable with digitally born scholarship?

JONATHAN: Absolutely. We struggled with this question. Ethical might be too strong of a word, but we definitely struggled with this question because Jackie and I both felt that as full professors, we have in some ways the responsibility to help other people in English studies broadly, in writing studies broadly, understand the value of multimodality. A print text was the best way to do that this time. I don't mean this in any arrogant way, but we have the luxury at this point in our careers to try to further the goal of getting readership for online presses, for digital presses, but part of that is making a broader community understand why multimodal work is valuable in the first place. The next project we hope to do together we'd like to be purely digital but then again you want people to read what you do and it would depend on audience. It's a tough choice for writing scholars to make.

CHRISTINE: I know at a Computers and Writing Conference I attended, I was in a session where we talked about this problem of citation. Writing scholars tend to cite print when working in print, and even when working in digital spaces such as *Kairos*, where I edit the Praxis section, still heavily cite print. In both environments it seems like authors don't always remember to go back and tap into those digital articles as sources. It's just not a two-way street yet.

JONATHAN: Which is unfortunate because I think some of the most interesting stuff that people are working with is in the online journals and I absolutely try to reference them to get the word out about what's going on in that work.

CHRISTINE: This is a related question because you do have your feet in a wide range of writing projects. Do you draw any distinctions in your writing life between creative projects, such as writing, say, gay poetry,

and then writing a scholarly journal article? You've got this range on your CV.

JONATHAN: [laughs] I definitely do.

CHRISTINE: Does your writing life differ based on the project?

JONATHAN: Let's see, how did it differ? My instinctual response, which is the one you want . . . [laughs]

CHRISTINE: [laughs] Yes, of course!

JONATHAN: Is I wish I had more time for the creative stuff. One of the things that Jackie and I have experimented with is the conference installation. We've done a couple of these for the Computers and Writing and Watson conferences. By creating a multimedia installation, that's an attempt to be both scholarly and creative at the same time. Of course, as soon as I say scholarly and creative, I feel like I've set up a binary, but I don't know that it really exists.

CHRISTINE: Yes. There's always that slash bar between them.

JONATHAN: I hate that divide because as I'm constantly telling my graduate students, I think scholarly work at its best is very creative, but when we think rhetorically, we sometimes view scholarly projects as separate from creative projects. Jackie and I wanted to try and blur the boundary a little bit more there and see if it's possible to do a combined project that is forefronting itself as scholarly—and forefronting itself as creative all at the same time. But otherwise, I do often think of creative and academic writing as somewhat separate kinds of activities, I have to admit—even in my own writing life. For example, I will backburner more creative projects if I have other scholarly projects that are a little more pressing. [sighs] That's how that goes.

CHRISTINE: [laughs] This is actually a perfect segue into time management questions. Like other faculty featured in the collection, you're being interviewed because you've managed to maintain a high level of scholarly productivity over many years. I see from a look at your CV, in several individual years you published a combination of articles, books, poetry, and might also spearhead a special journal issue. Is there some master plan of how you work on it all, juggle it, keep track of it all?

JONATHAN: Oh, sure. Absolutely. I keep a Word document that's called, literally, "to do." [laughs]

CHRISTINE: [laughs] Nice.

JONATHAN: T—o—d—o. I have it outlined usually by academic term. I have a section for summer and all of the sorts of projects I want to work on and try to get done this summer, and others for going into the fall, going into the winter and the spring as well. I try to forecast when I can reasonably get things done and, and start other projects and sort of layer and weave projects together. Of course, this plan always gets thrown because you might not get a manuscript back, you might have to do revisions that you hadn't anticipated. And editors are notoriously slow people. So my to-do list is always in flux. But just in terms of keeping track of the things that I'm working on, for me, the to-do list is really a matter of trying to move stuff off my plate. [laughs] I have certain commitments, so I'm trying to make sure to keep track of them so I can move them off my plate to get to other projects. I hope that's useful.

CHRISTINE: It is. When I conceived of this project I asked graduate students, other faculty members, senior people in the field, what are some things that you want to know about everybody's writing processes? Number one was time management. [laughs]

JONATHAN: The issue really is—it sounds so lame but it's true—just making writing a habit and planning for it.

CHRISTINE: Exactly.

JONATHAN: I've realized from writing for publication a long time that I can actually get things done even if I just do an hour or two a day. I actually work better, in fact. Believe it or not, I track my real productivity as a scholar with my movement into administration because when I became a writing program director, I all of a sudden had a lot less time [laughs] to actually do writing projects. So I realized that if I were going to continue to be active as a scholar, what I would need to do would be set aside specific amounts of time. My initial instinct was to try to set aside an entire day, like an eight-hour shot, and it just wasn't productive for me. What I stumbled upon that was much more productive was the one to two hours a day that I would set aside every day, and it's almost as though I just literally fell into that addicting habit. "Oh, it's this time of the day. It must be time to actually sit down and work on a writing project," as opposed to setting aside the eight hours in which I would fiddle around.

CHRISTINE: [laughs] Sharpen your pencils.

JONATHAN: Pet the cat.

CHRISTINE: [laughs]

JONATHAN: I had all of this ramp up to start writing because I had a full eight hours. While I said, "Oh sure, I'll get a whole lot done" about the eight-hour day, it wasn't true. It became much more effective for me to say, okay, if I do one or two hours a day, I will actually get more done because I'm much more conscious of the fact that I need to get something done during the short time period. It sounds crazy. [laughs]

CHRISTINE: No, it doesn't. In fact, Donald Murray even said one of the reasons short and regular writing works is because you don't need as much ramp up time—he likened it to "taking up an alien craft"!

JONATHAN: But I will say this about the long blocks of time. The long stretches of time are really useful for the kind of background reading and thinking that you might need to do and that's why sabbaticals are important. This coming sabbatical that I'm going to take, the year after this next, I'll have the entire year. For me that's crucial just in terms of having the stretch of time to think and to kind of read at will and to just explore and play. Those times are important even though they are rare, and I don't want to shortchange the importance of them. I use them to bank ideas, explore ideas that then during the regular academic year I can, I can develop into articles and whatnot.

CHRISTINE: One of the things you mentioned before was how you have a little bit of less time now that you have this administrative role. I wonder if you could tell me more about how your role as the campus writing coordinator connects with your own writing. For example, how has your own research on writing affected this role? Are there writing practices that you use as a writer that also are practices that you endorse or make a deliberate attempt to spread across campus?

JONATHAN: Sure. Everything we've been talking about in terms of the writing habit, developing a habit, remain absolutely important. When you first asked the question, it occurred to me that my administrative work often to me seems a little bit different than my . . . I don't want to say my intellectual work.

CHRISTINE: [laughs]

JONATHAN: I spend a lot of my administrative time doing WID [Writing in the Disciplines] and WAC [Writing Across the Curriculum] work. I spend a lot of time with faculty in the sciences and in engineering and in our business school and talking about developing courses for writing in their disciplines. On the surface, even I would say "Wow, this is really not a research area for me." I mean, I really don't publish in WAC and WID. But I've done writing assessment now for six years, and we have collected and scored over a thousand papers.

CHRISTINE: You must be exhausted! [laughs]

JONATHAN: It's this amazing archive, and I have a couple of colleagues who say, "Ah, you really should really publish in that. You should publish on that." And I've sat down a few times to kind of work on it and start the literature review on assessment . . .

CHRISTINE: And?

JONATHAN: . . . and to think about it, and . . . Christine, I love doing the assessment work, but it's not my scholarly interest, if that makes sense. I love the assessment work because I can see what it helps me do on campus and our curricula. We've made massive curricula revisions at my institution based on that assessment work, but I don't know that I want to contribute to that research area as a scholar. [laughs]

CHRISTINE: [laughs]

JONATHAN: [laughs] If that makes sense?

CHRISTINE: It does, and I feel your pain as a WPA [writing program administrator]. There's such a rich body of material, but [laughs] sometimes really you want to work your brain in other ways and think about other pieces in the field.

JONATHAN: Yeah, that's what I tell a lot of my graduate students. I say, "Look, as a compositionist, if you move into WPA work, you're going to end up doing a lot of things that will be really interesting, but you just may never write about them . . . it may not be part of your scholarly interest. Now, with that said, I have always been committed to interdisciplinary, and so there's another way in which my gravitation to WAC and to WID fits. As a WPA I've done quantitative, qualitative assessment. I'm working on an ethnographic project that will dovetail with the assessment work. Mixed methods and interdisciplinary, I would say are things that are very near and dear to my heart as a thinker, as a scholar, so it doesn't surprise me at all that I've gravitated precisely to those things as an administrator. Even though I never publish anything about WAC or WID, I'm energized as an administrator in dealing with those issues because WAC and WID really seems to be those moments in composition where we get to be really interdisciplinarians in some interesting ways.

CHRISTINE: You can research the writing, and even enact the research, without having to write about it.

JONATHAN: Exactly. [laughs]

CHRISTINE: If you were me, who would you interview in the field of rhetoric and composition about his or her writing habits?

JONATHAN: That one I'd want you to interview unfortunately we can't. I'd love to hear Susan Miller. She was a great mind, and she pulled ideas from so many strains of thought . . . composition and rhetoric, rhetorical studies, and philosophy. I would have just loved to have known how she managed to connect all of these ideas in writing.

CHRISTINE: She had a really amazing style too.

JONATHAN: Yeah, and I recently went back and reread "The Sad Woman in the Basement."

CHRISTINE: I remember that article.

JONATHAN: It's chilling in some ways. There's so much going on in that essay, and it's so ceaselessly suggestive that I felt completely inadequate as a writer. [laughs]

CHRISTINE: [laughs]

JONATHAN: I'm increasingly fascinated by those people in the field who really straddle both composition and rhetoric. For example, my colleague here, Susan Jarrett, for instance. She really is just top shelf both as a rhetorician and as a compositionist, and I think someone who has contributed in some transformative ways to both sides of that house as it were, to both rooms in that house, and has been able to make some interesting connections across composition and rhetoric. There are also a younger set of scholars, I think of Jenny Rice and Thomas Rickert, for instance.

CHRISTINE: Yes, I'm interviewing Thomas Rickert in a few months for this project.

JONATHAN: These are people who are wanting, and I think are intellectually equipped, to do both. They can produce compelling scholarship as both compositionists but also as rhetoricians. That impresses me, and I want to know more because I understand myself as a compositionist and as a kind of comp-rhet person, I don't really think of myself as contributing to rhetorical studies per se.

CHRISTINE: What makes you think so?

JONATHAN: I publish in *Rhetoric Review*, and the *Enculturation* piece is very much a rhetorical studies sort of piece, but I don't think of myself as doing that work.

CHRISTINE: It's hard to bridge both rhetoric and composition because both sides are growing larger by the day. I've asked several questions about this in the interviews to see how folks that do both types of scholarship navigate a balance. Anyone else whose habits you want to know about?

JONATHAN: Yes! The other people who kind of interest me are those people who have contributed substantially to writing studies but who themselves really loathe writing. [laughs]

CHRISTINE: I'm fascinated by those folks as well. I hear on a weekly basis how much I must love to write because I am a writing faculty member at my interdisciplinary faculty writing group. And I will say that in most of the interviews I have conducted so far, faculty do express a real joy for writing, albeit not every minute of the day.

JONATHAN: It's tricky because, and I don't think he'd mind me saying this, my buddy Scott DeWitt at Ohio State, is a case I'm fascinated with. He's somebody who published a wonderful book, had some great articles, but has shifted more towards doing administrative work, and really just doesn't write much. I've asked him directly, "You have such interesting things to say, why don't you put yourself . . . put your stuff out there more?" and he said, "I just hate writing."

CHRISTINE: [laughs]

JONATHAN: And so that interests me because I know he's a brilliant writing teacher, so that split interests me—the brilliant writing teacher who him or herself doesn't particularly care to write.

CHRISTINE: Well, his situation is part of the set up I'm using for this collection in the introduction. I'm going back to an early Maxine Hairston article in *Rhetoric Review* that talks about why writing teachers don't write.

JONATHAN: What does she say?

CHRISTINE: She speculates on some possible causes, and one of them is some writing faculty just don't like to write. At all. Writing faculty might love to teach writing and rhetoric and composition as a field works on the assumption that teaching writing and doing writing yourself are helpful practices when intertwined. But she notes there are

many writing faculty that still don't like to write even if they love to teach about writing.

JONATHAN: I would definitely put myself in the camp where my teaching and my writing are often going hand in hand. They are very interconnected activities for me. It's my administrative work that might seem like the odd person out, but even there, I think about administration a little more deeply because of teaching and writing. I can imagine teaching without writing, but I really can't imagine writing without teaching.

CHRISTINE: What's the difference for you?

JONATHAN: I write all the time about teaching experiences, teaching issues, problems and challenges. I usually write to help me understand better what I did wrong. [laughs]

CHRISTINE: [laughs] Well, and to possibly generate material for the next project!

JONATHAN: That's true. I always have new material from teaching to write about.

CHRISTINE: Do you have a project that you're going to work on for your sabbatical? Do you have something in mind, since you're going to get that larger block of writing time?

JONATHAN: I do. I'm actually undertaking a project on young adult fiction, and I'm very interested in how young adult fiction models different literacy practices and different media literacy practices for young people. In fact, this summer I'm teaching a graduate seminar on the history and theories of young adult fiction. I'm looking particularly at corporate sponsorship, to rip off of Deb Brandt, in literacies. What are the kinds of literacy practices that corporations are attempting to foster through young adult fiction? Young adult fiction is often transmediated, through something like *Hunger Games* or *Harry Potter*. The YA fiction is not just a set of books; it's a whole media franchise.

CHRISTINE: Absolutely.

JONATHAN: For me, the whole YA world just beckons, as it were. So many of these books stage teaching moments, and they themselves are about writing, about people using multimedia, becoming media literate, but then offer an interesting underpinning of material culture. Who's invested? I mean, YA literature is big business for a lot of people so I'm interested in how that whole corporate conglomeration understands itself and the work that it's trying to do. I'll inevitably critique that, but it's fascinating to me. I'm having a good time with it so far, and hope to get that writing project fully underway by the time I'm on sabbatical.

CHRISTINE: How did you get into this topic as your next idea for a project?

JONATHAN: This is actually, weirdly enough, work that is coming out of my administrative work. As my campus's writing director, I've had much more contact with community colleges and local high schools as these places have been trying to figure out how to better prepare their students for matriculation to our campus. So I had myself thinking a lot more administratively about those lines, those trajectories, and I became interested in where these students acquire their literacies including in spaces beyond the high school or community college classroom.

CHRISTINE: It sounds amazing to write about. I bet you'll have a great time working on it.

JONATHAN: Or maybe it's just fun to read young adult fiction. [laughs]

7
KATHLEEN YANCEY

KATHLEEN BLAKE YANCEY is Kellogg Hunt professor of English and distinguished research professor at Florida State University. Yancey has authored two books—*Reflection in the Writing Classroom* and *Teaching Literature as Reflective Practice*—and, with two colleagues, co-authored *Writing Across Contexts: Transfer, Composition, and Sites of Writing,* which won the CCCC Research Impact Award and the CWPA Best Book Award. She has also edited or co-edited another eleven volumes, among them collections focusing on portfolios (*Portfolios in the Writing Classroom* and *Electronic Portfolios 2.0*) and on assessment (*Assessing Writing across the Curriculum: Diverse Methods and Practices* and *Self-Assessment and Development in Writing: A Collaborative Inquiry*), in addition to other works in composition studies. She also co-founded the journal *Assessing Writing,* co-editing it for seven years. In addition, Yancey edited writing studies' flagship journal *College Composition and Communication.*

While teaching at institutions such as University of North Carolina at Greensboro and Clemson University in addition to Florida State, Yancey has taught over twenty different undergraduate courses, ranging from first year composition to English teaching methods and more than fifteen graduate courses, including visual rhetoric. Yancey has served as an administrator in varying contexts, including co-founding and directing the Inter/National Coalition for Electronic Portfolio Research. She has also served as president of the National Council of Teachers of English, Chair of the Conference on College Composition and Communication, and President of the Council of Writing Program Administrators. The interview took place on July 25, 2013, via Skype.

CHRISTINE: I'm doing your interview completely different than all the others because I have a great anecdote to tell you first and I'm going to use that to launch my first question.

KATHI: Sure. I'm ready!

CHRISTINE: When I was at the 4Cs conference this year, I was talking with a friend about this book project and asked her whose writing

DOI: 10.7330/9781607326625.c007

habits she wanted to know about. She said you. At the time, we were in a crowded hallway between sessions and out of nowhere this very intense looking gentleman just pops his head in between ours and says, "If you talk to her find out . . . " and then he looks around to make sure nobody is listening and then he says, in a scary whispering voice, " . . . if she ever gets writer's block?"

KATHI: [laughs]

CHRISTINE: So . . . Do you ever get writer's block? [laughs]

KATHI: Not in the way in which I think that term is usually used. I find some tasks easier than others but I think the key is that I'm never just writing on one project, and even if I were just writing on one project I'd have so much other writing to engage me. So you know you could have writer's block in a spectrum, right? On one end writer's block in this sort of originary genius version shuts you down completely.

CHRISTINE: Right.

KATHI: Then on the other hand you could have writer's block that was more, you know, intermittent, almost a part of the process. If you conceptualize it in that second way, I'd say sure and I think everybody has. For me . . . I like the beginning of a project. I *love* the beginning of a project. I find it energizing!

CHRISTINE: [laughs]

KATHI: One of the questions that you have on your list [of potential questions passed out to interviewees] is whether I revise and if I like revision and the answer is generally speaking, yes. I actually see myself as a reviser and it's taken me a long time to get to the place where I really think I'm engaged with the craft of revision. I think that's an acquired skill. But the mental part from shifting from a few good ideas to getting started . . . that can be really hard. And then there are sometimes places in the middle where I know something's not working but I don't know what it is, and then what I tend to do is just flip to something else. I've always got something else going on. So I'll go do the something else or I'll take some kind of a break and then I'll come back. I've never had writer's block in the sense that you know you're spending, I don't know, weeks or months or even days on end unable to write. I think writing is in my DNA.

CHRISTINE: Can you explain what you mean by that?

KATHI: For me, I breathe, I write. I mean, whether it's writing to colleagues or friends or family members or something that is more work related, responding to student work, whether it's in a class or a dissertation or a thesis or writing letters for people, which I seem to do a lot or writing in connection with *CCC* you know . . . It's ubiquitous. It's all the time. And that's before you think about texting, for example, which I seem to do more and more of.

CHRISTINE: Well, now this gentleman has his question answered so there you go! [laughs] You actually had said something that was going to

be one of my later questions, but let's get to it right now. Where you talked about how your writing habits have changed over the years, you mentioned you've definitely gotten more in tune with revision. So, I wondered if you could say a little bit more about that. Perhaps something that you have noticed as a writer that has developed over time for you?

KATHI: Sure. I think I was always pretty responsive as a reviser. But really within the last five years I get a lot of pleasure out of, not every single revision, but I like how William Gass talks about "makingness" of a text, and I like the makingness of a text. I like working with words. I like working with document design. I like working with visuals. I like making all of that come together in a composition. And I like different kinds of compositions. So, that's one change but the other is embedded in that comment. I mean, it's really about the visual. What I usually say is that I became aware in the 1990s of two strands of research. One had to do with the language that people were using to describe computer activity, ICT.

CHRISTINE: Right.

KATHI: And it was located in architecture. So, I decided if, really, if I wanted to understand this I should understand a little something about architecture and I literally went to Borders bookstore now in demise . . .

CHRISTINE: Yes, so sad.

KATHI: Dating me as I go forward evermore. [laughs] And I picked up a book by Bernard Tschumi. Now I didn't understand at the time that he was the dean of the architecture school at Columbia. But he was at the time.

CHRISTINE: A new area for your research?

KATHI: The thing is, it was about postmodernism in architecture. So rather than do the conventional thing which I suppose is to do the cannon to start with, the Greeks or someone around there, I chose a way in that was familiar to me because this book was on architecture and postmodernism and I knew something about postmodernism.

CHRISTINE: Reading in context helped you link those two fields together?

KATHI: Right. When beginning into architecture study you don't just talk about architecture, you don't just read or write about architecture. It's very, very visual, right?

CHRISTINE: Absolutely.

KATHI: And that connected with the second strand which had to do with the research on people who were very creative, such as Picasso, who were able to function in more than one modality. Picasso obviously is an artist but he was actually quite articulate in explaining his perspective to the public, and one of the reasons we know him, I think, is because of, in part, that ability to communicate. And I thought,

"Well isn't that interesting?" If I wanted to be smarter, it might be wise to know something about the visual. Pretty soon after that I went to Clemson, and the college that houses English also houses architecture. I ended up doing a lot of work with graduate students in architecture and it just changed the way I see the world. I began doing more and more talks with slides that I really thought of as a blank canvas.

CHRISTINE: Almost as prewriting technique, would you say?

KATHI: There's no question. It's a source of invention for me. There's no question about that. It is absolutely a source of invention for me. Now that doesn't mean that necessarily every single project starts that way, but a lot of projects that I engage in start that way. I also think that comes in part from doing a lot of workshops and giving a lot of talks. Workshops are more interactive so it's not stand and deliver . . .

CHRISTINE: [laughs]

KATHI: Right? A lot of times you want to focus people's attention and an image can be the way to get their attention. I've found that I really [laughs] *really* like the visual. I really like using visuals in my writing. That's the reason I'm kind of hesitating when you ask if it's prewriting. Yes. It is. There's not a question. It's a source of invention. But it's also a modality that I call on in writing and it is very uncommon for me to have a piece of writing that has no images.

CHRISTINE: That leads wonderfully into my next question. What I try to do before these interviews is read selections from the person, really try to get a sense of their writing habits and how articles are put together . . . essentially the architecture of them. I noticed your pieces stand out from a stylistic standpoint but also from a delivery standpoint. I know delivery itself has been an area of research for you. Do you feel there is a relationship between the subjects you're writing about and then how you actually write about them?

KATHI: Hmm. The relationship of form and content.

CHRISTINE: Pretty much. To distill it down.

KATHI: Yeah. Sorry, I went to the Walmart version.

CHRISTINE: [laughs] That's all right. Maybe this collection will end up having lots of Walmart comments throughout the book to make great copy for the book jacket on the back!

KATHI: That's it! I think the short answer to your question is yes. But I'll say that it's complicated because as much as we tout desktop publishing and the role of the author etcetera, when it comes to incorporating images, when it comes to document design you know you work with publishers and some of them are more hospitable to these kinds of requests than others. I'll say that.

CHRISTINE: True.

KATHI: My 4Cs chair's address was reprinted in Bedford's St. Martin's books on the 4Cs chairs' addresses and this brings up a second issue. I really worked with 4Cs to get that formatted the way I wanted it.

And I had the help of somebody who was very sympathetic. Marilyn Cooper, who was the editor of the journal at the time, and Rona Smith, who is the production manager at NCTE, and both of them were terrific in terms of helping me think through what I wanted to do. And how I could make that text do what I wanted it to do. But notice the number of people who are involved. Bedford's St. Martin's is wonderful. I think their reprinting of the 4Cs chairs' addresses was a lovely thing and Duane [Roen] did a great job. That said, the address wasn't the same. They were more interested in reprinting.

CHRISTINE: Yes. A historical document almost.

KATHI: Right. Except of course that it's not a historical document . . .

CHRISTINE: Because it's not how it actually was meant . . .

KATHI: Well, it's not how it was. In part it's not how it was because there are images that I could publish in a nonprofit journal like *Cs* that they wouldn't release or the permissions or whatever would cost too much.

CHRISTINE: I see.

KATHI: And so I had to swap out images.

CHRISTINE: That is an interesting conundrum.

KATHI: Right. In answer to your question, I do actually think that form and content are related and . . . I think I gravitate toward questions around how much room am I going to have here to do what I want to do. This also, I have to say, assumes that I'm writing by myself.

CHRISTINE: This actually raises a really good question. You've collaborated with several different people. How does that work for you? Do you pass drafts back and forth via email? Are you physically together with your co-authors when you write? What are your collaboration strategies to make sure academic writing is completed?

KATHI: I just identified five people that I've collaborated with within the last two years. I've written with a lot of students over the years. Or ex-students. So, I have a piece coming out with Matt Davis who was a grad. He's now at UMass Boston. I have a book coming out with Kara Taczak and Liane Robertson who are also alums. Let's see and during that time . . . And I wrote a piece with my friend and colleague Kristie Fleckenstein, and Matt and I did a piece together and that's only within two years. At one point I did a count before I had written with some of these people and I had collaborated with over twenty people.

CHRISTINE: That's amazing.

KATHI: Happily not all at once! [laughs]

CHRISTINE: Boy that would be crazy wouldn't it? [laughs]

KATHI: Yeah. Exactly! Now I think about collaboration work differently. It really depends on the group and the size of the group. A partnership, generally speaking, is easier than let's say five though I've written with as many as seven. It really depends on whether each of you is going to do the whole draft. How are you going to start? Is one of you going to draft one section, another of you is going to draft a different section, then you're going to swap? Or is somebody going to do basically a concept and then another person is going to take that concept and run with it and then swap it back and forth? When you swap back and forth are you going to use track changes or are you going to give people permission to overwrite your prose and you won't know where they changed it? I mean, different people feel differently. And also you can write with the same person again and that person or you may feel more possessive about the prose than you did last time around.

CHRISTINE: That's true, and that's something that no one else has brought up in an interview when I've asked about collaboration. Some writing faculty have a set person that they write with, and they've established ways of doing things, and they've just managed to just make that work. There's not really a discussion there about how you might be a different writer the next time around because you now have had more experience and influence from your past co-authors.

KATHI: Truly you may really care more. I mean one of you may care more. Sometimes there are practical issues. It's a question of how much time one has. And especially where it's a situation where . . . like when Brian (Huot) and I were editing *Assessing Writing*, we were also writing some other pieces. We co-edited a book together and then we did some other book chapters for other people and then we were writing introductions to the journal. That was a situation where we asked who's got the time to do what. Or who feels that a given topic is someone's strength.

CHRISTINE: It's a negotiation.

KATHI: I think there's a lot of that kind of negotiation among [rhetoric and composition faculty] and I also think collaboration works better where both people, or even in a larger group, really are able to see what the text itself needs. If you have that agreement going in then it's really fun and interesting. It can be frustrating too, but I do think you get a very different kind of text because you have more brain power working on it.

CHRISTINE: The collaboration may result in a totally different way of approaching a topic.

KATHI: Yes. That's exactly right. I wrote a piece with Teddi Fishman that's in Amy C. Kimme Hea's book on wireless technologies. Teddi and I are friends and we've done a lot of stuff together, workshops and that kind of thing, and it was really fun to write with her. In part it was really fun because she is so smart and just came to that topic in a really different way than I did. That perspective made the piece much richer as a consequence. It's much more than anything I would have done on my own. I think that's part of the pleasure of it. In that situation you're not only sharing what you think you know or you're exploring what you think you know, but you're learning from someone else in the process and it's just really wonderful.

CHRISTINE: Do you have someone in the field of rhetoric and composition whose writing you admire?

KATHI: Doug Hesse. He thinks of himself in some ways as an essayist, and when you look at his writing you can see why. He is somebody who knows the craft of writing and is very adept at evoking the reaction he wants for an audience. It's a nice match between an ability that he's honed over time and something that is not just intellectual contribution to the field but provides that contribution with an aesthetic that's pleasing. Louise Rosenblatt described this as bringing together what she called the "efferent and the aesthetic." Nancy Sommers is another.

CHRISTINE: I love her writing. I use it all the time in a lot of writing methods classes.

KATHI: She's another one who really works at it, her craft. When you read it or when you hear her read it, it doesn't feel that she worked at the writing because there's such congruence. Going back to your earlier question, between the form and the content the writing feels almost as though it were effortless. But I know that it's not.

CHRISTINE: Speaking of effort, you're a very busy person. You're editing the *Cs.* you've been the chair of most of our national organizations. You're directing your graduate program. You've been the interim chair. You've got a lot going on! How do you manage to make time for all this writing? You're putting out several things a year and it's very consistent. How do you get the writing done?

KATHI: When my kids were little they took a lot of time, but I'm pretty focused. And I have to say I think I really like writing. It's not an obligation. A lot of what I understand comes through writing. When I have a lot of things going on and I can't make sense of them, I tend to want to write about them because through writing about them I can at least wind them up and begin to get the items to talk to each other. That's one way that I write. I start getting interested in something and I do a lot of reading, and I do a lot of writing. When I'm finally ready to sort out "what does this mean," I have to do something by way of writing to find it. I think I have a lot of strategies.

CHRISTINE: Do you write on paper, or write on the computer? What does your composing process look like?

KATHI: There are times when I kind of leap up and I go to the whiteboard in my office because I need a shared space where I can make sense of something. Sometimes I will sketch something out on a piece of paper. I almost never write something without having some kind of paper around me. But in terms of drafting, I don't draft longhand. I draft on the computer. I tend to mark each draft and I can tell you that I have, generally speaking, at least nine drafts. They're not complete drafts because draft two may have had some changes that I just didn't save, right?

CHRISTINE: Right.

KATHI: You can't save every change you make. It's a process. And then maybe about draft four or five I print it out. And the reason I do that is that the screen landscape won't allow me to get a bird's eye view. And I need a bird's eye view. I'm a big picture person.

CHRISTINE: The smaller issues get masked by the screen space?

KATHI: Right. Well, and I tell you if you're using images and you're really trying to work with formatting to make certain points, you have to do that because otherwise you can't tell what the overall pattern is. There are also times when I might be mulling writing over on the drive in to school and if something comes to me, if I were to think of something that is wrong or an addition or a question I have, it's not uncommon for me to call myself. [laughs]

CHRISTINE: [laughs] I've done that! Do you have a writing schedule or a ritual?

KATHI: I have some rituals. I don't have a schedule because I travel a lot. When I'm not traveling, I try to find a morning or better yet a day. Even a morning would be good. I tend to write on Saturday mornings and I tend to write on Sunday mornings. Not always, but frequently. When I travel I'm really good at getting a lot done. I can write in an airport.

CHRISTINE: I've actually heard that a lot. Some people say they get their best writing done there because they can't be bothered by anybody else.

KATHI: And I write on planes. I do. If my husband and I are doing a road trip I can write in the car. [laughs] But if I say, "Okay, this is a writing weekend" that doesn't mean . . . I will brush my teeth, okay? [laughs]

CHRISTINE: [laughs] Sweatpants?

KATHI: Oh yeah!

CHRISTINE: And coffee?

KATHI: Oh, a lot of coffee.

CHRISTINE: [laughs]

KATHI: I guess that's my way of saying that for me, I like routine but I'm really a spurt person. So I need some routine but if all I had was routine, honestly I think that would be counterproductive for me. I like a big swath of time when I can think about something, do some writing, get up and do some laundry, come back and do some writing, do a little email, get up and do something else. I like that sustained attention. That really makes writing happen for me. When I get in the flow I don't want to quit, especially in summer. If I get cranking at 10:30, I can just keep going. I can just keep going until the little cranking machine runs down.

CHRISTINE: Right. Until you're done. Your body knows you're done and you're finished.

KATHI: That's right. I'll come back to it but I need that swath of time. For me, it's more of a balance between structure and routine that enforces or encourages writing and then big blocks of time that allow me to sort of disappear into time.

CHRISTINE: I've found one thing from these interviews is that everybody does it differently. Joe Harris talked about how he really likes that like one- to two-hour block and then if he has to think about something he would like more time for larger projects. Yet Cindy Selfe writes in these teeny-tiny pockets all day long in five or ten minute slices. But others write from 8:00 to 9:00 AM all seven days a week with the attitude "I just do my hour a day and I'm done."

KATHI: Oh no. I could never do that! That would feel constricting.

CHRISTINE: And academic writing is not the only type of writing that has to be worked into a day.

KATHI: It's really a question of what is the contribution you want to make at this moment in time. A friend of mine said to me a long time ago after I edited a couple books, she said, "you know there will come a point where you will want to write more than you want to edit." [laughs] I really like editing. It gives me a lot of pleasure. I like working with authors. And I think that it's a different kind of contribution to the field. So I've really enjoyed it. But I will say, five years is plenty. [laughs]

CHRISTINE: Yeah. [laughs] It's like chairing a department, right?

KATHI: It's fine and you've done your bit and now it's somebody else's turn. And that's good for the field. And the field gets a different take. The journal does a different kind of, a somewhat different kind of work probably, than it did before and then you can go back to doing more writing if that's what you want to do. Or other people make different choices. Other people decide that they want to do something in administration. The good news is there are many opportunities and all of them are going to require writing of some kind or another. The question is, you might say, what kind of writing is the writing you want to dominate your schedule right now?

8
CHRIS ANSON

CHRIS ANSON is distinguished university professor and director of the Campus Writing and Speaking Program at North Carolina State University. Previously, he spent fifteen years at the University of Minnesota, where he directed the Program in Composition from 1988 to 1996 and was Morse-Alumni Distinguished Teaching Professor. Anson has received numerous awards, including the North Carolina State University Alumni Association Distinguished Graduate Professor Award, the State of Minnesota Higher Education Teaching Excellence Award, and the Morse-Alumni Award for Outstanding Contributions to Undergraduate Education. He has received or participated in over $1.8 million in grants. Anson has published sixteen books including the popular textbooks *A Guide to College Writing* and the co-authored *Longman Handbook for College Writers and Readers*, and over 115 journal articles and book chapters and is on the editorial or readers' boards of ten major journals. He is also a former chair of the Conference on College Composition and Communication and president of the Council of Writing Program Administrators.

Over the course of his career, Anson has taught a variety of courses in composition pedagogy, writing across the curriculum, writing program administration, and writing for teaching. In addition to currently directing the writing program at North Carolina State, he has previously held other administrative positions such as co-director of the Teacher Training program and coordinator of Advanced Composition at University of Minnesota. The interview took place on August 13, 2013, via Skype.

CHRISTINE: When I started working on the idea for this collection, I asked a lot of graduate students and faculty colleagues whose writing practices they would most like to hear about, and your name was one of the ones frequently mentioned.

CHRIS: Really? I'm amazed.

DOI: 10.7330/9781607326625.c008

CHRISTINE: Yes, and I think I understand why. You've published a hundred plus journal articles, fifteen books, and just generally had a prolific academic writing career. The writing is consistently published year in and year out after looking at your CV. Is there something you've always wanted to write about that you haven't gotten to?

CHRIS: Well, I did my first MA at Syracuse in creative writing. My plan was not to become a university professor. I wanted to be a novelist. That's where my interest in academic writing really began, surprisingly, in the creative writing realm. I got drawn toward the study of writing at Syracuse. I was really interested in how people write, and that kind of sucked me right in to composition studies, and so I kind of put on hold, the really creative work until maybe I retire. [laughs]

CHRISTINE: [laughs] I hear that a lot actually.

CHRIS: What I've done, what I've managed to do, I think, is try to approach some things within the profession a little more creatively. So I've written lots of scenarios for example. I did a whole book of scenarios on writing across the curriculum, where I edited a bunch of other people's scenarios and then added one in each of my own in each of the chapters. If you look at my CV, I've been involved in scenario writing for faculty development for a long time, and those are kind of like bad fiction. [laughs]

CHRISTINE: [laughs] And that's where the connection between creative and academic writing lies for you?

CHRIS: Yes. So I did this early work in creative writing and then put that on hold and tried to build some creativity into some of the more academic things that I wrote along the way. But getting back to your question, if there's one thing I really want to do it's write a novel eventually. In the short term I also have a piece I've been working on for several years, which I want to get finished. It's an article on the transfer of writing ability across contexts. It's kind of a *tour de force,* but I just have to get finished with it because a lot of other projects have gotten in the way. That's a more immediate "want to get done" project.

CHRISTINE: You mentioned the faculty development angle. I run several workshops for faculty on how to become more productive writers. I notice you also offer writing workshops for faculty on how to integrate writing in the classroom. Are you able to pass on your own successful writing habits in these venues? Are you able to get your identities as a faculty writer and a faculty developer to connect?

CHRIS: Occasionally, and there is a lot of potential for collaboration there. In most of those workshops the people there are really interested in what they can do to integrate more writing into their courses without driving themselves crazy. There's a lot of stuff on assignment design and grading—how do you become an efficient and consistent evaluator of students' work? When faculty members' own writing comes up, we talk about how they do have expertise that they can pass on to their students. Faculty often don't realize that because they're not used to thinking of themselves as practicing writers who have something to say about writing.

CHRISTINE: **As a writing program administrator, I've run similar workshops and come to the same realization. Faculty often see student writing and their own writing as separate enterprises.**

CHRIS: That may be because in a lot of faculty development we don't talk about writing, about our own writing. That used to be a staple in the Toby Fulwiler and Art Young kinds of workshops early on where people wrote a lot; they wrote whole texts during the workshops just to understand how students would struggle. It's an interesting concept to think about—how much more we can talk about our own writing in those settings.

CHRISTINE: **Would you say that this discussion happens more in graduate seminars focused on composition theory?**

CHRIS: It often comes up, and I also do a whole session on writing and publishing and how to be productive at academic writing. I have a little shtick on that and then we talk about what the students' own practices are.

CHRISTINE: **What are some writing habits that have worked for you that you are passing on to your students?**

CHRIS: I've learned that if you leave a project open on the screen and never either minimize it or put it away in a folder, I've found that whenever you open up the computer to do something else, that piece is sitting staring at you. As soon as you put it away, as soon as you put it into a folder, or close it down, it's gone, and you have to force yourself to go reopen it. It can be gone for days as you work on other things, but it's never gone if it sits on your screen,

CHRISTINE: **Can you explain how keeping the writing on screen actually gets you to work on it?**

CHRIS: Sometimes I'll find myself, if I'm doing email or something else, seeing that text and seeing a sentence in it and sort of diving back in. Then the next thing I know I've spent an hour pushing it forward. This is a fairly recent strategy for me. Since I have forced myself to leave things open on the screen, and because I do almost all my work on the computer, I tell students to try the strategy of leaving writing open on screen. Just make sure you never put it away. You can move another window over it or something but leave it there so there's a constant reminder that there's a project waiting for your attention.

CHRISTINE: **Cindy Selfe mentioned that she does that same thing so that she can work on a writing project or do video editing in those tiny little pockets in your day when you have five minutes between student conferences or meetings.**

CHRIS: It's really amazing how much you can get done in just a few minutes. You can do some stylistic work if you're tired, and if you don't have much time you can tinker with something minor. You can more easily drop in a reference to something you've been reading. Just working for a few minutes does end up moving [the writing project] forward and I think psychologically always entering into your consciousness and so your mind is maybe sort of subliminally working on it all the time.

CHRISTINE: Are there other productivity strategies you use to make sure projects get finished?

CHRIS: When I first started as an assistant professor, I had meetings every six months with the chair of my department who was a pretty good mentor. He really wanted to make sure that untenured people had time to write. He told me to stay home on Fridays and work, but one of the things I started doing that I shared with him as a part of this process, and one he was really impressed with, were tracking grids. I started making these grids that tracked projects from either an early idea or a conference paper all the way through to eventual publication. I started filling these grids out thinking "I've got to keep pushing each of these things forward until it gets out in print," and these also served as maps for writing days.

CHRISTINE: And once the project is published, it falls off the grid and is complete?

CHRIS: There were spaces on the grid if the writing was turned down to note how to rework some of the ideas and then send it to another journal. Again, the writing is never put away until it is published. It's almost like a flow chart. When my colleague Deanna (Dannels) arrived here, she was a brand-new assistant professor and was working in the program that I direct. I think she looked upon me as a mentor because she asked me how to be productive. I showed her these grids and said this might be something you want to try. I forgot about the conversation until four or five years later I was in her office and noticed there was a grid on the wall of her office. I said "Is that one of those grids?" and she said "Yeah, I took your advice and I started creating these grids," and so I said "Has it worked?" and she said "Oh yeah, it's fabulous!" She even had color coded things. [laughs]

CHRISTINE: It's great to see a how a specific productivity strategy actually works when another person tries and adapts it.

CHRIS: She's very productive and actually mentored another student whose committee I was on. Deanna was really mentoring this student much more than I was, and the student finished up and went to the University of Kentucky as an assistant professor of communication. When I was visiting to do a program review there, I saw this former student in her office. When I looked on her wall, and there was one of these grids! [laughs]

CHRISTINE: [laughs] It's catching on. What did you say?

CHRIS: I said, "That's one of those grids, does that help?" She said, "Yes, I'm tracking my publications and making sure my projects get finished!" I've now seen firsthand how faculty who track writing, in whatever style they like to use for those flow charts, grids, or whatever, works because there is a constant reminder where things are in a bigger picture sense, not an individual project sense.

CHRISTINE: **You noted you even start a line on the grid with just an idea to write about or as a possible conference proposal. How do you actually get in and start one of those writing projects? How do you get it from idea to first draft, or outline or . . . ?**

CHRIS: What I find myself doing a lot of is what I call semi-drafting, and it's a kind of freewriting, I guess. It's somewhere between the sort of real Peter Elbow-ish anything goes freewriting and more focused freewriting where you do have an idea, but you're writing your way in. I do that semi-drafting even when I'm doing pretty consistent work on articles. Even with a draft of an article, I won't yet have all the answers; I won't have all the references. Or I need to consult some research, so I'll draft, and as I'm drafting I'll put in bracketed comments like, "get such and such" or "insert such and such here," and so it looks like it's got partially some text that's usable. I'm actually trying to write the text, but it also has all these sort of interpellations with my commentary, that are the semi part, that are the "maybe you need to do this or what if you do?" . . . it's sort of an on-going commentary to myself.

CHRISTINE: **Why do you think semi-drafting works to get you from idea to more finished product?**

CHRIS: I find that, first of all, that semi-drafting informalizes the writing. It makes the writing process feel less like you're under pressure. Secondly, I think it puts these place holders in that as you're working, you remember you need to do certain things. Getting back to the idea of keeping the text up on screen, I'll look at it and I'll see one of those bracketed comments, such as "go dig up such and such," and I will go dig that up. Or I've got five or ten minutes and I'm going to go get that reference I noted was missing in a bracket.

CHRISTINE: **This semi-drafting strategy seems to make good use of faculty time. You can semi-draft in longer pockets of time and deal with the brackets in shorter pockets.**

CHRIS: Yes, this seems to work for me because there are all of these cues in the text for me to do those smaller things. The brackets are almost like a to-do list or reminders inside the text itself. I tell undergraduates to try to semi-draft because I think they believe that the better you get as a writer, the more able you are to pour effortlessly, pour these sentences out into a text, and I say that's not the way writers work.

CHRISTINE: **[laughs] Teaching how to use brackets for items to tackle later might be a good strategy for undergraduate writers who might have trouble juggling the tasks of maintaining momentum of writing about a single thesis but also minor tasks such as finding a source or wanting to use a stronger transition in a paragraph.**

CHRIS: I think the brackets in a draft work well also because you want to see where it is in the text that you need to do something. I don't use a whole lot of the sort of traditional prewriting strategies, cluster diagrams, those kinds of things, because I kind of do that within the text.

CHRISTINE: You mentioned getting advice to take Fridays off to write or otherwise protecting writing time. Do you say once I've completed an hour of writing I'm done? Does writing informally happen as long as you have a writing project on your screen?

CHRIS: The writing is pretty constant. I'm always writing. [laughs]

CHRISTINE: [laughs]

CHRIS: I mean, there are so many writing type things stacked up. There's a P[romotion] and T[enure] review that I have to do, there's an article I'm working on, there's something else I have to do like review for a journal, and those types of writing projects come in all the time. I'm almost always working on a review for a journal because I review for seven or eight journals, so there's always an article sitting, waiting to be reviewed. And then students' PhD dissertation drafts need comments. This writing is different than writing an article or a book chapter, but it's all writing, so I'm always shuttling between those projects almost all the time unless I'm doing something like preparing to teach.

CHRISTINE: How do you manage these other types of writing that are your own projects for publication?

CHRIS: I use an electronic tracking system for what is due when on my smart phone, and so I'm constantly opening that up and feeling really good when something's done. In fact, the first thing I do when I finish a review is go to that thing, and erase that item. [laughs]

CHRISTINE: Erasing an item probably feels great. [laughs]

CHRIS: The problem is that stuff is going on there as fast as it's going off, so it never ends, so the writing is really pretty constant. It just depends on what it is. I think the fear that I have is that there are so many smaller things and so many responsibilities to other people that I won't get the long, sustained writing time for my own writing projects. Getting back to your question about time, I do have to force myself to say I'm going to take an hour; I'm going to work on this article. It's just the constant flow of the work that makes writing for publication a challenge for faculty.

CHRISTINE: This is switching gears a little bit, but since you're obviously well connected and have written a lot yourself, whose writing do you admire in the field?

CHRIS: I like writers who really craft their writing. I think too often we forget as compositionists, we want to be writing really well in addition to researching well. The field admits a really broad range of styles from almost clinical, empirical research, to more analytical stuff and interpretive stuff, such as case studies, to work I think of as being really highly crafted. The language itself becomes really important. I think of writers like Deborah Brandt. I was always impressed with how hard she worked on getting the writing right with herself, to get it to read really wonderfully. I also think of Mike Rose in that context; his writing is just so fluid and so readable, wonderful and rich in that creative sense.

CHRISTINE: Do you model your own writing off of these writers you admire?

CHRIS: I find myself moving along a continuum, and I think I've probably learned to adapt different styles to different occasions, but sometimes I'm sort of disappointed with the writing that I have to do when it's more empirically orientated and less lively. But I've seen people do empirical writing effectively such as the Andrea Lunsford and Bob Connors's "Ma and Pa Kettle Do Research" article. [laughs]

CHRISTINE: [laughs]

CHRIS: That essay was a perfect blend of "Look, we're doing a really big, a really important research study, but we're going to write this in a way that's not the really typical, dull social science-oriented piece. We're going to be lively in it; we're going to joke around a little bit." I just love that. I don't think we do that enough as a field, but again I think it depends upon the occasion and the context. I like when writers take chances within the scholarly context.

CHRISTINE: What is something no one knows about you as a writer?

CHRIS: Oh boy!

CHRISTINE: [laughs] Anything you want to share?

CHRIS: Well, something that's invisible when you're only looking at final work is what happens along the way. I think one of my failures as a writer is that I can't go on until I get the sentences right. [laughs] And so I'm probably working on the first parts of papers more so than the later parts. I mean, I just obsess. I keep reading and rereading, tinkering and rereading until I can move on, and that can be a problem. I think Don Murray said, "Don't get it right, get it written," and I've never followed that advice. It *is* great advice. But I just cannot bring myself psychologically to push ahead into the piece until I'm really happy with what's already there, and so my writing contains this constant recursiveness.

CHRISTINE: Can you describe how that works?

CHRIS: I tinker and tinker with a sentence or paragraph until I think, "Uh-huh, that sounds pretty good, now I'll move ahead and do some more."

CHRISTINE: Anything else that might surprise readers about you as a writer?

CHRIS: There is another thing. I love to write and so people talk about me being a born English major because I was writing when I was really young, but one thing that many people don't know is that I actually learned to write in the 1960s using a quill pen, a plastic pen with a little metal quill tip that's replaceable and inkwells in the desks at school.

CHRISTINE: Oh wow. [laughs] That is a fun fact. Where did you learn to write?

CHRIS: I was going to a French-speaking public school in France where my family lived for about six years when I was really young, and we had to wear these little frocks because we couldn't spill the ink on our street clothes. This also sounds medieval, but the teachers came around and filled little ceramic inkwells that were in these little depressed things in the desk. We all had these little quill pens and we wrote with ink. We dipped those things into the inkwells and wrote. [laughs]

CHRISTINE: What an amazing tactile experience.

CHRIS: And so I think of that famous article by Janet Emig called "Hand, Eye, and Brain," the hand part was an inkwell and I had to learn to make sure that I had just the right amount of ink and this is just a really bizarre memory of early writing for me. Now I can hardly write anything by hand anymore that's legible to anyone except me, and sometimes even I can't reread it. [laughs] Everything I'm writing now is done on computers.

CHRISTINE: Do you ever print out any drafts? To make comments or edit?

CHRIS: Yes, I do. My wife and I have a beach place on an island off the coast of North Carolina, and we will go out and sit on the beach. I can read my writing in text form and I can get sand and sunblock on [the print copy], and it won't make any difference, right? [laughs]

CHRISTINE: [laughs] Right. A little beach reading.

CHRIS: So, I get to do some work out there with a pen, right? It's just not on the computer.

CHRISTINE: Is there anything else about your writing that you would like to share with us? Is there anything you think as the field we should be doing about our own writing as faculty?

CHRIS: I've been really taken with some of the work of Elizabeth Wardle recently, and folks like Doug Downs who study writing about writing curriculum. I'm interested in some of the concepts behind that, like this notion of mindfulness. I think we need to keep working with students on getting them to be more aware of what's happening when they write, and we need to study our own writing practices as faculty. I mean, it's exactly what you're doing for this book project—essentially bringing to consciousness the writing habits and dispositions of writers so other writers are able to figure out which writing behaviors are self-defeating and which of them are productive. If students say "I compose best when I've got a can of Diet Dr. Pepper, my headphones on with my favorite music," I'll say, "Well, you feel pretty comfortable doing that, but why don't you try something a little bit different and see if it works better? Try not having any music on or try doing something in complete silence." Then students can see if they can't write, music actually does help them, but they should know the difference between a productive strategy and what might be unproductive or self-defeating writing habits.

CHRISTINE: Or even just a habit. You think you need to do that, so you do it.

CHRIS: I've also been rethinking procrastination a lot lately as a writing behavior. I've always admonished students, "Don't put writing off. Do it. Start early," but a lot of people are telling me that they actually need the mental adrenaline rush that comes from a deadline that's looming. They say they do their best work when they're really hypercharged because they've got to get it done, and I don't think we've explored that possibility very fully. We just assume that people don't do good work when they're doing it the last minute.

CHRISTINE: Also pushing someone to start early may not account for needing a longer time to mull over an idea before writing. Writing teachers might frame it as procrastination but a student might be reworking an idea for several weeks in their head and really thinking about it before they get to the point where they have to write. It doesn't mean the idea for the writing wasn't developed or thought about prior to starting.

CHRIS: Janet Emig talks a lot about the subconscious writing that happens when the writer is not actually writing. I can relate. I think I was incubating the CCCC's address for a year [laughs] because I was thinking about it on my runs and I was thinking, but actually I didn't start it until about three months before. I think it was there in my mind as an upcoming very high stress rhetorical situation for many, many months, and so I don't think I wasn't doing anything. The address was sort of turning it around and around in my head. I think mindfulness or rhetorical awareness that Downs and Wardle and Emig talk about can help writers, including students and even faculty, bring reflective habits of mind to their work. I like that direction the field is taking, where we're helping writers to learn more about what we do in the field instead of just getting them to do it, so that they have a meta-awareness of what's happening as they write.

9
DUANE ROEN

DUANE ROEN is professor of English at Arizona State University (ASU), where he currently serves as dean of the College of Letters and Sciences, dean of University College, vice provost, and coordinator for the Project for Writing and Recording Family History. At ASU he has also served as director of Composition and co-director of the graduate program in Rhetoric, Composition, and Linguistics. Previously Roen served as director of the Writing Program at Syracuse University and was founding director of the graduate program in Rhetoric, Composition, and the Teaching of English at University of Arizona. Roen is former president of the Council of Writing Program Administrators, former secretary of the Conference on College Composition and Communication, and former co-editor (with Greg Glau and Barry Maid) of *WPA: Writing Program Administration.* In addition to more than 280 articles, chapters, and conference presentations, Roen has several books including: *Composing Our Lives in Rhetoric and Composition: Stories About the Growth of a Discipline* (with Theresa Enos and Stuart Brown), *Views from the Center: The CCCC Chairs' Addresses, 1977–2005,* and *The McGraw-Hill Guide: Writing for College, Writing for Life* (with Greg Glau and Barry Maid).

Roen began his career teaching English at New Richmond High School in Wisconsin, where he served as high school language arts chair and K–12 language arts chair. While there, he taught a range of courses in composition, reading, creative writing, and cultural diversity. At the postsecondary level he has taught a range of undergraduate and graduate courses, including first-year composition, writing methods, language methods, linguistics, writing program administration, composition theory, writing assessment, portfolio assessment, discourse analysis, writing for educators, literature for adolescents, and the Nebraska Writing Project. Roen's interview took place on December 13, 2013, via Skype.

CHRISTINE: Let's start with a question I've never asked anyone in interviews so far. How do you *feel* when you write?

DOI: 10.7330/9781607326625.c009

DUANE: Well, that depends. When I write for publication I have a much different feeling than when I write for work. When I write for work I write a lot of reports; I write a lot of proposals. In my job I write close to one hundred emails, on average, a day. When I write for work there is a different feeling, since much of the writing is routine and doesn't require a lot of creative thought. But when I write for publication, I think about a lot of things. It's escape from my day-to-day work routine. And when I'm writing I'm able to just forget about anything else and I really focus. For example, if my wife walks up behind me and says "hi," I jump because I'm so focused on what I'm doing. I have a lot of positive thoughts and feelings associated with what I'm writing when it is for publication versus work.

CHRISTINE: What contributes to these positive thoughts or feelings?

DUANE: I'm sure I have a lot of positive associations because writing for publication, for a project I want to work on, is such a nice change of pace from writing memos and reports and composing email messages and reviews. But I also really enjoy spending time on writing for publication.

CHRISTINE: It sounds like you do a lot of writing during your day. Can you describe when academic writing time fits into your schedule?

DUANE: My ideal would be to write every day when I get up at 5:00 AM. However, when I get up every morning at 5:00, I have a ton of emails waiting for me and some need immediate attention. On weekdays I do all administrative and teaching work from about 5:00 in the morning until 5:00 PM at night. Then I go home and have a quick dinner and then I get upstairs in the study and write for publication.

CHRISTINE: Does your writing schedule vary on the weekend?

DUANE: Yes, it is more my ideal. Saturday and Sunday I'll just get up at the same time and just start writing because I don't have as many administrative and teaching tasks so I get to them later. So, I am a daily writer but it varies from weekday to weekend day when I actually start writing.

CHRISTINE: Can you describe one of these typical writing sessions? When you sit down to write, what do you do to get yourself started?

DUANE: It depends on where we are, and I say "we" because I co-author most things that I write for publication, and if you ever want to co-author anything let me know.

CHRISTINE: [laughs] We should! That would be fun.

DUANE: Because I co-author most things, early drafts are done in Google Docs. When I start a writing session, I want to back up a little bit and see where I am with a piece, and going into Google Docs helps me see where my co-authors and I have left off.

CHRISTINE: Even though you write daily, is it difficult to find a place to start writing or does looking at the Google Doc for a project help?

DUANE: It does help orient me to where I need to work. However, one of the most challenging parts for me is to find out exactly where I want to go in the piece of writing so there is a little of that "writing to discover," that Don Murray thing. But a lot of it is writing to discover in very rough prose, as fragments, and bullet items. Then once I know where I want to go with this chapter or article, everything starts to fall into place. Once I have that rough outline I have a better feeling of where I want to go. So again, it depends on where I am in the process when I'm writing.

CHRISTINE: **Do you write in a linear fashion once you have that outline?**

DUANE: No, I jump around quite a bit. So this morning I might wake up and decide that I want to work on this section of this chapter and then later in the day I might decide that I want to work on another section. My mind gets a little weary working on a section, then I do a load of laundry, let's say, and that perks me up because just changing to that new section refreshes me. Any change of pace refreshes me. And by change of pace I mean when I write, and then do laundry, just that few minute break is enough for me to get invigorated and keep writing.

CHRISTINE: **Is it hard to get back into writing another section once you've left it for a few days to work on something else?**

DUANE: Occasionally, but because I have a rough outline I generally know where to pick up again, even though I need to spend time writing to discover what I want to say. It's a very recursive process.

CHRISTINE: **Did you ever have a project that you were working on that was particularly challenging and you had to really gear yourself up for writing or push through the difficulty to sustain momentum?**

DUANE: One thing that comes to mind immediately are my textbook projects. Textbooks are, in my experience, the most difficult, challenging kinds of writing projects to do.

CHRISTINE: **How so?**

DUANE: One, you have so many reviews, you have dozens, sometimes hundreds of individuals giving you feedback that needs to be taken into account as you revise. Another thing is that a textbook project is so big. At one point, one of my textbook manuscripts was up to three thousand words and we had to cut it down to about two thousand words. And that project went on for years as most textbook projects do. So that's probably the kind of writing project that requires the most stick-to-it-ness and persistence to complete.

CHRISTINE: **How do you keep yourself motivated to persist through the writing of such a large project? Is there a trick you use to stay on track when the end of the project might not be for a year and a half?**

DUANE: Yes, while I'm writing I try to only think about what I'm writing right now. Right now I'm working on a handbook project that has seventy-one chapters. My co-author and I just finished going through the seventy-one chapters again, doing this one certain revision to all seventy-one chapters. For me it's sort of like getting into the zone or a Zen type of experience where the act of doing it is sort of relaxing, satisfying, and comfortable (maybe comfortable is the word). And so I just do it. That has been my philosophy about a lot of things. There are some types of things that I like doing more than others, including some writing tasks I like more than others. My attitude has always been just like the Nike ad—to just put on your shoes and do it.

CHRISTINE: [laughs]

DUANE: To me, that satisfying feeling is enough motivation: the act of doing something that needs to be done and working towards the goal, even if the goal is a lot way off. I find that comforting and satisfying.

CHRISTINE: I'm sure a lot of struggling faculty writers would want to know how you get yourself to have that good feeling when you write, if that makes sense. Are you ever able to convey that notion that academic writing is a satisfying endeavor in any way to graduate students who are kind of lagging in their own big projects?

DUANE: Sure. When I direct dissertation projects in particular, I talk about my own writing and especially my writing related to my book projects. I talk about how I do the writing I do every day; the daily discipline that I have. They don't always hear about how faculty actually write and get things published so I try to make my own writing transparent.

CHRISTINE: I bet sharing your own writing practices makes graduate students more aware of how much work is entailed in academic publishing. Articles don't happen out of nowhere.

DUANE: I think that, maybe I'm fooling myself here, but I think that telling them my own habits gives students some confidence and gives them some reassurance to do these kinds of projects. They see they can actually finish something large like a dissertation, and faculty do this type of writing throughout their careers, so it can be done.

CHRISTINE: Is there a specific project you tell them about that works well as a model?

DUANE: I recently talked to a group of freshmen students about one project. I do a lot of family writing workshops throughout the Phoenix area. I talk about the daily journal that my wife and I have kept since October of 1978, and we now have more than fifteen thousand pages in that journal. We didn't write those fifteen thousand pages all at once. My wife and I have written those over thirty-six years now, and it's fifteen minutes a day. If you think about it that way, fifteen thousand pages, oh my word, that's a whole lot. But if you think fifteen minutes a day set aside for writing, that's nothing. This is the way that I get students to think about getting writing done: write every day and set a goal for yourself.

CHRISTINE: What type of goals do you advise?

DUANE: I talk to them about setting a goal of so many words. I used to say just set a time; for example, you're going to write for a minimum of an hour or a half hour. But I find that there are some people who get distracted during that half hour. So I say set the goal of, say, 250 words a day and stop when that's done if you want, or if you're excited, write more. I ask students "Does writing 250 words a day sound reasonable?" Everyone agrees it is reasonable. Then I point out if you write 250 words a day, in half a year you have 180 pages, which is a pretty good-sized dissertation project. Dissertation writers then feel the project isn't so big or insurmountable. And so I like to talk to writers in those kinds of ways.

CHRISTINE: Since you've written these large projects, how do you approach revision in your daily writing sessions? Do you go into a section saying, "Okay, I need to revise this section"? Does revision happen kind of automatically as you go? Or is it a more deliberate activity separate from the writing to discover you mentioned earlier?

DUANE: It varies. Right now I'm co-authoring an article about names and the rhetoric of names. What I find myself doing in this case, as I've done in other cases, is as I re-read what I've written I find that I want to add something or make some kind of change. But then there are other times where the main thing I'm working on is revision. For example, on the handbook I'm working on, we went through the seventy-one chapters and found that each chapter needed the same kind of changes. This revision was almost formulaic and did not require intense thinking once we figured out how to do it the first time. So in that case we went through the chapter without focusing on really anything else in the chapter. It really varies depending on what we need.

CHRISTINE: Does your revision process differ when you are looking at one of your smaller projects in a Google Doc?

DUANE: Google Docs is amazing for revision. When I'm in Google Docs and I'm writing or I'm revising and then one of the other co-authors updates the draft in Google Docs and I see what that person is writing, it spurs me to change something that I'm working on as well. We can revise at the same time and spur each other on. I do think the drafts are stronger because we can see incremental changes as they happen.

CHRISTINE: You raise an interesting point about your collaborators and how they affect your own writing for revision. How has one, or more, of your collaborators influenced your writing specifically?

DUANE: One example that comes to mind is the *McGraw-Hill Guide.* When we did the first edition, that was the book that had the 3,000-page manuscript at one point. Sometimes I or another author would feel a little weary, but then another team member would sort of step up and take charge on either revising a chapter, and that would help the other collaborators feel more energized. That's one thing that I've learned is that team members can re-energize one another and spur a project on to completion.

CHRISTINE: Has anything else changed about your writing as a result of collaboration?

DUANE: There are some writing habits that have been certainly reinforced by collaborative writing. Sometimes I'll work with someone who adds something that needs to be added and will put in the margin "cite later," and that can create difficulties because they forget what the citation should be. This practice kind of reinforced for me to provide the full citation *now,* because I know that it's easy to forget where things come from. So that's one thing which seems little but may cause a larger problem later on. I think there are also probably some stylistic things affected when I co-author works with another person. For example, I begin to notice certain stylistic features of their writing. Seeing how someone else's writing is structured will also spur me to use stylistic techniques that are not natural components of my writing style. And by stylistic, I should add I mean sentence structure, word choice, that kind of thing.

CHRISTINE: In your long history of academic writing, you've done a lot of articles, books, textbooks, everything. Is there a piece that you are most proud of?

DUANE: I think that the *McGraw-Hill Guide* is pretty good. I just finished co-authoring something with Nick Beam and Sherry Rankins-Robertson on how we as academics should all be public intellectuals. I think that that is supposed to come out in *Academe* this spring, and we make a good argument. Even though the editor had to cut it back a bit to get it to fit into the issue of *Academe,* and it wasn't ideal, but I think it does a pretty good job making an argument we want to make.

CHRISTINE: And totally different types of writing which contribute in different ways to the field. Is there anything else that you'd like to add about your writing process that I didn't ask before?

DUANE: Yes, I don't consider myself any smarter than anyone else, but I do consider myself really self-disciplined. I think that self-discipline is important in order to publish regularly as a faculty member. I believe the *Framework of Success in Postsecondary Writing* [Council of Writing Program Administrators] and the postsecondary habits of mind are documents that show what it takes to succeed as a writer, and I think I have some of these habits of mind described in these documents that make me a productive writer. When I work with student writers, one of the things that I try to convince them is you don't have to be brilliant to be a productive writer, but you do have to have these good work habits. I like to instill that idea in the student writers that I work with.

10

CHERYL GLENN

CHERYL GLENN is university distinguished professor of English and Women's Studies at Penn State University (PSU), where she is John Moore teaching fellow, director of the Program in Writing and Rhetoric (PWR) and co-founder of PSU's Center for Democratic Deliberation (CDD). She is the author of *Rhetoric Retold: Regendering the Tradition from Antiquity through the Renaissance*, the first extended history of rhetoric inclusive of women; and *Unspoken: A Rhetoric of Silence*, the first rhetoric of silence, and the forthcoming *Feminist Rhetorical Studies: Essays on a Field of Dreams*. She served as the 2008 chair of the Conference on College Composition and Communication, and in 2009 she was named Rhetorician of the Year.

In 2015, Glenn was elected to be the inaugural president of the Global Society for the Study of Women in Discourse and Rhetoric. She co-edits two book series and has published prize-winning articles; many chapters; a widely adopted writing pedagogy text (now in its eighth edition); and numerous textbooks on grammar, research, and writing (also in multiple editions). Her research, teaching, and mentoring have earned her numerous honors and awards, including three grants from the National Endowment of the Humanities and best article awards from *College Composition and Communication* and *Rhetoric Review*. Before coming to Penn State, she taught for eight years at Oregon State University. Glenn's interview took place on September 13, 2013, via Skype.

CHRISTINE: I recently interviewed Jessica Enoch about her writing habits, and she credits a large part of her success as a writer to having you as a writing role model. What writing habits do you practice that you try to also instill in your students? Are there some set strategies that you tend to give all of your graduate students or undergraduate students to help them become writers?

CHERYL: Well, that's a good question. So much of what I do seems so natural now because I've been teaching so long. My graduate students and my undergraduates have been really successful; I'm so proud of them. I

DOI: 10.7330/9781607326625.c010

wouldn't take credit for any of their success, but I would say they're all successful. I think I get the best graduate students . . . that's why!

CHRISTINE: [laughs] Well, Jessica and I had a wonderful interview, and I know she credits a lot to you.

CHERYL: Let's start with that. Of my graduate students, six of them have won national dissertation awards, so I think that says something about what great writers they are and what great writing habits they have. Five of them have won the CCCC's [Conference on College Composition and Communication] dissertation award.

CHRISTINE: That's amazing.

CHERYL: I think that says a lot for them. All of them wrote in dissertation writing groups which I have formalized here at Penn State, and I run two or three dissertation writing groups a semester. They're not all my students. The students have to get permission from their advisor to join a dissertation writing group, and we learn how we work together to read and respond to one another's work. So, the idea that they have work due on a regular basis I think helps them write.

CHRISTINE: They learned the techniques it takes to get to publication early in their graduate careers.

CHERYL: I think Jess would probably say that one thing she learned from me is to get a rough draft. It doesn't matter how bad it is; just get it out so you can start revising and not be prideful about that first draft . . . and to write every day. I don't write on the same project every day, but I'm writing on one book project or another every day because of deadlines. I think what Jess sees and my other graduate students see is that I'm in the office, and in between meetings I'm writing. Many professors don't come to the office, as you know.

CHRISTINE: [laughs] I do know.

CHERYL: I come every day unless I'm traveling, of course. I travel quite a bit but otherwise I'm here every day and this is where I do my writing. And I think that's a good habit, which means that it's rare that I write at home. If I don't go home until 7:00 o'clock, when I go home, I'm ready for a big glass of wine.

CHRISTINE: [laughs]

CHERYL: And then I get up at the crack of black, I go to the gym, I go home, take a shower, and come to the office and I write all the time in my office. I think that's unusual but there's nothing mysterious about it so students see me writing. Even when they come in, I'll say, "Just let me finish this sentence and let me write down what I was going to say next," and then they wait for me for a minute. Then I go over and talk to them so they see how I learn to interrupt my writing, make a note of where I'm going next, and then I'm able to come back to my writing.

CHRISTINE: It's a trick all future faculty really need to learn . . . how to get started writing again.

CHERYL: I think watching someone write could be a good habit. Watching someone like their professor write is a good experience for them. And I think writing and revising together is a really good experience for graduate students too and gives them a lot of support as they move through graduate school and into the profession.

CHRISTINE: I know one of the things that Jessica and I talked a lot about was just this idea of letting students see you writing and making that writing process very visible, and she mentioned studying how you wrote. So that's very cool to see a mentor and a mentee practicing the same habits and passing them on through the chain of the profession.

CHERYL: I would say too that in my graduate seminars I also have a series of sequential assignments that build on one another, and I think [this series] shows students how to go about building a big project like a dissertation. Most of my seminar assignments end up being an article, a conference presentation (that would be the least of it), but an article or a dissertation chapter, so they see how to put that [type of writing] together too, and it launches them.

CHRISTINE: You are someone that's managed to balance both scholarship in rhetoric and composition, and I just wondered if you could say a little bit about that balance. There are faculty that identify more strongly with rhetoric and some more with composition, and that comes out in the scholarship. In your case I see a bit of both, so I wondered if you could talk about that relationship a bit?

CHERYL: I can. When I started out I wanted to be only a rhetorician and only a historiographer, and I did composition studies because it was expected of me and I enjoyed it, but I thought at that time, when I was young, there was more prestige in being a rhetorician. That's very frank.

CHRISTINE: That's not at all unusual from what I'm hearing.

CHERYL: I've worked in composition all along, and I realized that my work in composition is another one of my feminist rhetorical goals. If my professional goal is to make rhetoric more inclusive and more representative of all the people who use language purposefully, I want them to be able to use it effectively as well. If that's one of my goals, if I want to make sure that I recognize that performances and the potentials of women I started researching—historical women, contemporary women—then I already started working on [research about] people who inhibit subaltern groups. I'm so happy that I realized, maybe ten years ago, that one of my feminist rhetorical goals would be to make sure that all sorts of people knew how to write and had access to power, prestige, effectiveness, agency, and they could establish that access through writing. So, it was a beautiful moment when my feminist goals, which had been anchored in rhetoric, suddenly connected with compos-writing studies in a really self-conscious, purposeful way.

CHRISTINE: I have a related question about feminism. You are cited as one of the feminist role models in the collection *Women: Ways of*

***Making it in Rhetoric and Composition.* One of the things I was surprised to learn about you is that you admit that in your first faculty position at Oregon that you struggled with publishing. That's a concern that's heard from many faculty across disciplines. In the time between then and now, you've obviously established some very strong writing habits, and we've talked a little bit about these habits. Could you say a little bit more about the transition to becoming a more prolific writer? Was there a time that it suddenly became clear to you that you needed to do certain strategies to write more effectively or was there a shift in your thinking?**

CHERYL: I would say that what happened at that time was very much [sigh] contextualized. I was going through a divorce. I had a young daughter. I had just moved cross country. I was alone. I had a very heavy teaching load. If I could get supper on the table every night and get five hours' sleep, I was really happy because I had a lot of students. I had not yet established a feminist rhetoric historiographic methodology, which I did establish in my first scholarly book, *Rhetoric Retold.* I had these personal pressures which didn't allow me much time.

CHRISTINE: But you managed to figure it out.

CHERYL: At the same time, I had no methodology, and by that I mean no way to read the materials I had. I had good research methods. I still am a pretty good librarian and archival researcher, ethnographer, field researcher. I'm good at all my research methods but I had no methodology. Nobody had any methodology for me to use, so it took me several years to develop a feminist, historiographic methodology, a lens through which to read my materials and write my work, and once I had that I was off and running.

CHRISTINE: That makes sense. If [a methodology] just isn't there, you don't have the next way to proceed and there's only so much researching you can do if you don't have a clear direction as to where you're going to go.

CHERYL: Well, and how to read the material. Remember this was very early on in feminist rhetoric work, very, very early on. All my students have a methodology now. So they have a head start. Or they have a fair start, I should say.

CHRISTINE: [laughs] I hope you don't mind me asking this. Can I ask you an academic couple question?

CHERYL: Sure.

CHRISTINE: I am also part of an academic couple, and I've realized through a series of these interviews how many of us are there. I just interviewed Thomas Rickert yesterday and we talked a lot about this relationship. Since you are part of an academic couple, do you ever have, say, writing study dates where you're writing near each other or you're getting the benefit of being in the academic couple for your scholarship?

CHERYL: [laughs]

CHRISTINE: [laughs] I don't know how to say that in a better way.

CHERYL: It sounds so beautiful.

CHRISTINE: Doesn't it?

CHERYL: This is what I imagine all other couples do. I just think all other academic couples just cozy up on the sofa with their laptops and just sit there and write. We don't.

CHRISTINE: [laughs] Neither do we, if it makes you feel better.

CHERYL: The best we do is we are each in our own studies. I don't find that very conducive. Really, I like it that we're both academics. I like it that—I really love it when my husband reads my work, which isn't often enough, but maybe earlier on in our marriage we did that. We've been married a long time. It's what I think every other [academic] couple does, but we don't.

CHRISTINE: Is there a dream project that you've always wanted to work on but you haven't done yet?

CHERYL: Well, I want to finish the book I'm working on now called *Field of Dreams: At the Intersection of Rhetoric and Feminism.* The ways that rhetoric has much to teach feminism about reaching an audience . . . about establishing ethos. And feminism has a lot to teach rhetoric about justice, equality, inclusivity, invitation. Those sorts of things. So that's the book I'm working on, and it's a dream book. The book I'd love to do that I—and I have a contract for it—and I've told them I can't do it but they've been holding onto it for years, is a new edition of Ed Corbett's *Classical Rhetoric for the Modern Student.*

CHRISTINE: Oh, I would love it if you would redo that. I use that it in my classes. I love his work.

CHERYL: Of course. We all do, and it's the book on which all the others like that are based. Oxford [University Press] would very much like me to take on a new edition of that. I think I could do it and have a lot of fun doing it, and I think I would do an okay job. I wish I had time. That's the project I would most love to do.

CHRISTINE: That's ambitious!

CHERYL: And, you know, I love him. There's a picture of him up on my wall. When I rotated off as chair of CCCCs [Conference on College Composition and Communication], I got lots of presents, including a beautiful picture of Ed Corbett.

CHRISTINE: Revisiting his *Classical Rhetoric* would be a great project.

CHERYL: Yes, well, if you could just get me some time!

CHRISTINE: You just get busier. That's the life lesson.

CHERYL: I'm lucky, aren't I?

CHRISTINE: Very lucky.

CHERYL: Because some people don't have project after project after project. I'm really lucky.

CHRISTINE: Is there anything else you want to add about faculty writing?

CHERYL: I admire those people who just write. I do, but the older I've gotten, the more I've felt that my writing life is very, very important to me, but if my professor from thirty years ago comes by and wants to spend the evening, I'm not going to do any work. I'm going to spend it with him and his wife, and those are the decisions that I find myself making more and more, and it's a real luxury to make those kinds of decisions. So I love my writing life. I write a lot. I admire all my friends who do, but if you come through and want to go to dinner, I'll turn off my laptop and go to dinner with you.

11
MALEA POWELL

MALEA POWELL is a mixed-blood of Indiana Miami, Eastern Shawnee, and Euroamerican ancestry. She is chair of the Department of Writing, Rhetoric, and American Cultures at Michigan State University, and former director of the Graduate Program in Rhetoric & Writing, as well as a faculty member in American Indian Studies. She is past chair of the Conference on College Composition and Communication and editor emerita of *SAIL: Studies in American Indian Literatures.* A widely published scholar and poet, her current book project, *This Is A Story*, examines the continuum of indigenous rhetorical production in North America, from beadwork to alphabetic writing.

Powell previously worked at University of Nebraska–Lincoln where she taught American Indian literatures and rhetoric seminars. In her current position at Michigan State, she has taught courses in both technical writing and rhetoric. In her spare time she hangs out with, in her words, "crazy Native women artists & poets, and does beadwork." Powell's interview took place on January 30, 2014, via Skype.

CHRISTINE: You say on your LinkedIn profile: "I'm a mid-career academic, a published scholar and poet and editor and mentor of graduate students and a disciplinary leader who's winding her way towards becoming a romance writer and a beadwork artist." You are making and doing a lot of stuff. Where does writing fit into the picture?

MALEA: I think I've been pretty consistently in the process of trying to figure that out. Early in my career I took writing for granted because I'd always been a good writer in school. I never really had a lot of problems generating ideas. I'd been trained as a poet, and I actually think that helped me not to be worried about what I was doing with my writing. Then when I started to first shift to administrative writing, and then later I started to shift towards romance writing, and I would say in the last couple years I've become really aware of just how tenuous our grasp of what we do as writers really is.

CHRISTINE: [laughs]

DOI: 10.7330/9781607326625.c011

MALEA: [laughs] Here's what I mean. I feel really solid when I'm writing an academic article. I feel like I know what I'm doing, and then to learn how to be a romance writer has taken me all the way back to being a beginner. I have to figure out not just what the industry expects but what the genre expectations are, how to do them well, the difference between what I think is a good scene and what the people might think is a good scene . . . all the things that as an academic that I'm really just not worried about because I have found my groove.

CHRISTINE: Has your writing process changed from doing the academic articles to romance writing? Or is the process still the same, but just harder because you are starting over?

MALEA: I'm suddenly finding, you know, that my odd predilections, [laughs] and my own preferences make it hard for me to get rid of some pretty bad habits I think that I have as a writer. It's been really humbling to take on a new genre at this stage in the game and to be treated by other writers like what I really am, which is a beginning writer.

CHRISTINE: Tell me about some of these bad habits as a writer. [laughs]

MALEA: What I learned when I first started working on the romance manuscript was that I have a tendency to write in pieces, and while that can be really advantageous to sort of piece scenes together, I don't have a lot of patience with the kind of what I call the squishy in-between stuff. In an academic article that's not a problem because there's not a space for squishy in-between stuff, right? It's more straightforward: "Here are four things I want to say. Here are the moves I'm going to make." By the time I make them, that's as long as it can be. And in a novel you know readers expect more. [laughs]

CHRISTINE: In a romance, readers want a little more buildup or transition probably. [laughs]

MALEA: They do. All that connective tissue becomes really important, and I think it's one of the differences between a good genre novel and a bad one. I'm also writing a scholarly monograph right now and seeing the difference between academic writing and romance writing. I'm relearning a lot of things about writing that I teach students but that I think I'm exempt from. And I'm not. [laughs]

CHRISTINE: [laughs] No one is. Tell me a little bit about this manuscript that you're working on.

MALEA: This is the biggest mess I've ever made in my life!

CHRISTINE: I can't wait to transcribe that sentence. [laughs]

MALEA: So the punch line for the book is that I argue for a continuum of rhetorical production across kinds of making in indigenous cultures, anchoring one end in the sort of literary and autobiographical writings of the nineteenth century and the other end with contemporary native artists and people like basket makers and bead workers. My big argument, which isn't much of a reveal for folks of native studies, is that native people are engaged in consistent rhetorical practices across forms of making.

CHRISTINE: What's so messy about this project, beyond possibly the scope?

MALEA: If I had just kept it to the doing the textual readings and doing the oral histories with the artists and combining them I would have been fine, but I made the classic researcher error and I gathered too much data. I spent three months last summer going to every single place that these books had been composed in and following the path, mapping the path they made geographically and spatially. I audio recorded and then transcribed all of that, and now I've realized I can't make the first argument without bringing space and place into it, but there's no way to make that kind of complicated argument in under two hundred pages in a way that I think is coherent.

CHRISTINE: Is this problem specific to writing about native studies?

MALEA: When we start talking about traditional native artists who do things like make baskets, or do crow work, place figures in some really sort of literal ways, right? The materials come from a specific place. They're located somewhere. The tribal groups have a relationship with them so I figure, "Well is this connection between space and artifact an argument that I can make about the writers?"

CHRISTINE: Thinking about the space where an object is composed does add another layer to how we talk as researchers about how others write.

MALEA: My book has gotten me to think we don't have very good ways to talk about our writing as writing faculty. I'm happy about this project you're doing because I think that we have to talk about our writing in some pretty honest ways for a long time before we start to develop a good vocabulary. And we need to share this information with PhD students. I'm teaching a newly developed graduate writing class in the spring. We're going to require it as part of our core where it's not a writing for publications course. It's really a writing course.

CHRISTINE: How do you want to design this course since it sounds like you are breaking new ground?

MALEA: I want to try to take what we know is good writing pedagogy, not just in first-year writing, but in creative writing and songwriting and digital writing, to take what we know are good practices in those spaces where we have expertise and bring them to bear on the kind of writing tasks that graduate students find themselves faced with such as exams and dissertations but also letters of recommendation and administrative writing. What I care about is how can we teach them to be more rhetorically flexible but also give them a place where they can practice without judgment, without having to worry about turning it into a publishable piece, where they can make a big mess and then, you know, learn from that mess in a way that has some guidance? This is classic me. I take the thing I'm the worst at and then I design a class to address it. [laughs]

CHRISTINE: We also have this type of class in our MA writing curriculum at Findlay, but at the doctoral level it seems essential to prepare future faculty members (assuming they pursue faculty positions). I know from running faculty writing groups that many new faculty are hastily learning how to write on the job, and even writing a strong letter of recommendation for a student is a genre no one has taught them to do. We workshop a lot of these letters in addition to prepublication drafts.

MALEA: A graduate writing course is essential, especially because of the pressures that the [academic job] market and promotion and tenure put on faculty. I think that we rarely talk about our own writing difficulties unless we're talking to a friend or a writing group participant or close colleague, yet we sometimes expect our students to be better at writing than we are. Many graduate students in rhetoric probably placed out of first-year writing.

CHRISTINE: Do you talk about your own writing difficulties with students or colleagues?

MALEA: Oh yes, I'm not ashamed to say publicly the book is a mess. It's a mess. I made it a mess on purpose and we'll see if it ever comes out. What I'm worried about at this moment is if it's legible to anybody else but me.

CHRISTINE: What other kinds of writing challenges have you had since you might want to work them into your new graduate writing class? [laughs]

MALEA: [laughs] I have a list. I think that I struggle with a lot of the same things that other people struggle with. I struggle with things like motivation. I frequently struggle with how to chop giant ideas down to size. I think the hardest thing for me these days is finding writing groups that are productive for me. I've tried really hard in the last couple years to join writing groups and to be a good participant in them, and I'm having less luck than I would like at getting feedback.

CHRISTINE: What do you think the problem is?

MALEA: What I want from someone in a writing group is I want to get pushed, right? I can send a poem to a critique group and whoa, do I feel pushed. Yet I send a [scholarly] article to a critique group and I don't feel that people want to push. That's what I've been trying to do in the last couple months is try to find folks who are willing to push me because everybody needs to have their thinking pushed, no matter how successful or old they are in the discipline. [laughs]

CHRISTINE: Do you write every day?

MALEA: This year was the year that I decided that I was going to take myself in hand. [laughs]

CHRISTINE: [laughs] How so?

MALEA: I've made myself build some rewards into following structures that I already had built to be more productive and so now I have very set days when I do particular kinds of writing. I write every day, but I don't do research writing every day. Part of that weekly structure is because I was starting to feel like all the writing that I was doing for my administrative job was invisible even to me because it was mixed in with everything else I did in a day. And because I want to visualize it for my colleagues in merit and promotion, I want to make it visible to me as well. And so I do write every day, but those days have very different writing foci. And so Monday is an administrative writing day and so any tasks that I have that require me to write things get done that day. Tuesday's a teaching day [laughs] so no writing gets done. Wednesday is a research day. Thursday is a research day. Friday is a day that I do some prep writing. I try to make lists of where I need to be on particular projects and then I can work on that on Saturday. I don't work on Sundays. That's one of my new, concrete rules. I have a year-old granddaughter.

CHRISTINE: You have to draw the line somewhere! A new granddaughter is a good reason. It sounds like you've made establishing specific times for writing the reward.

MALEA: I don't work when I get home anymore either. I used to come home at 6:30 PM and then eat dinner and write, but I don't do this anymore because my relationship with my husband and being able to see friends are things that feed me much more intensely than a constant stream of work can feed me.

CHRISTINE: It sounds like defining when you write has led you to being more productive. You can see a high level of productivity from a quick glance at your CV.

MALEA: I've tried to rethink how I want to publish so I am productive in a way that is satisfying. In my early career, I never managed to successfully collaborate with anyone, so one of my goals after I got tenure was to do some collaborative work with people, whether that was collaborative essays, collaborative research, whatever. What my CV will end up looking like in five years is really radically different than what it looked like before. I have a lot more collaborative work now; some of that with grad students, some of that with colleagues. I even have some collective work where I did this 1960s idealist "let's all eight of us get in a room and write collectively!" thing. It took us a year and a half to write an article. [laughs]

CHRISTINE: [laughs] But you had the luxury of time and tenure to try something like that.

MALEA: Exactly. And talk about learning about yourself as a writer and as a human being. Collaborative writing together in the same room is one way to do it. Oh my! [laughs]

CHRISTINE: [laughs]

MALEA: That type of writing is what mid-career is for in my mind. I know that a lot of my colleagues think mid-career should be pushing towards full professor, and that's all fine and good, but really I think my work is going to get more varied and more experimental. There's going to be a lot more installation work and a lot less published print work. And that's because I think product ideas come to me all the time so I want to make sure that I don't just leave them in the dust. I don't want to leave something behind that I'll regret. And I don't want to be engaged in doing work that I think is not interesting just in order to get the next rung on the ladder.

CHRISTINE: Yet you have hit a lot of the rungs. You recently finished the stint of being the chair of the 4Cs [Conference on College Composition and Communication]. Serving as chair is a major milestone for anyone in our field, and it has come at this period in your research and writing where you're extremely productive.

MALEA: I think that my entire attitude towards the discipline has changed radically from that experience. I feel like things that I used to think to be true either got proven or disproven. So, I no longer have paranoias. I have some facts about tendencies that I see, and I also understand where the spots are to dig in and do some work and make some change. I feel really lucky to be able to do that through my work as chair but I think in terms of my personal scholarly production, man . . . I just did my annual review and girl, it is wrecked!

CHRISTINE: [laughs] Oh no!

MALEA: It's one of those years where everything's in the pipeline and nothing is published in a given year. It looks wrecked but it's not really wrecked. You timed this interview so well because I just finished my annual review and could review where I want to go. What I know now is my work will take on two really distinct projects focused on changing disciplinary paradigms. One around histories of rhetoric, which is no surprise. But the other around education and graduate pedagogies, specifically how we teach graduate students, not just how we mentor them.

CHRISTINE: What about your focus on native studies?

MALEA: My scholarship in native studies is going to use multimedia more often. I'm working on a digital archive project with some literary history scholars. I'm going to keep working on another project with native artists. As a result of using more multimedia, my only publication last year was not a publication; it's a contributing artist gig at an installation which is different from past scholarly work. I think that those types of projects seem really different. To me, they seem really complementary to what I'm already interested in. But, I think as a writer I'm headed toward genre fiction. I like that group of people. I like that community. That's a place for me to grow and change as a writer even as I reach retirement age. I've learned a lot about how to talk about writing.

CHRISTINE: Yet, you teach and do academic writing as a rhetoric and writing faculty member.

MALEA: What being in romance writing groups has taught me is that we're not very open about sharing our writing in the discipline prior to publication. It's nothing to belong to an online group where you've never met anyone face to face in the romance industry and exchange chapters and drafts and critiques. Nothing at all. That's normal. That's usual. That's how you get in. That's how you learn the business. But we don't do that in rhetoric and writing. We do talk about our writing in private little ways inside programs or between collaborators or among alum of a certain program, but you couldn't just go join an online group and be pretty secure that no one was going to steal your idea and pretty secure that you were going to get good advice and not advice that's based on someone else's benefits. In our discipline we just don't have a culture of that type of sharing, despite all of our talk about the importance of peer workshopping. Any talk about writing in our discipline is so local in nature. I'd like to see that change.

12

HOWARD TINBERG

HOWARD TINBERG, a professor of English at Bristol Community College, Massachusetts and former editor of the journal *Teaching English in the Two-Year College*, is the author of *Border Talk: Writing and Knowing in the Two-Year College* and *Writing with Consequence: What Writing Does in the Disciplines.* He is co-author of *The Community College Writer: Exceeding Expectations,* and *Teaching, Learning and the Holocaust: An Integrative Approach.* He is co-editor of *What is "College-Level" Writing?* and *What is "College-Level" Writing? Vol 2.* His publications have appeared in a variety of journals, including *College Composition and Communication, College English,* and *Change.* In 2004 he was recognized as US Community Colleges Professor of the Year by the Carnegie Foundation and the American Council on Education (ACE). He is a former chair of the Conference on College Composition and Communication.

At Bristol, Tinberg teaches four courses in the fall and five in spring which include first-year writing, an English literature survey, and an honors seminar on the Holocaust. In addition to teaching, he is currently serving as chair of the Faculty and Staff Senate. His interview took place on September 13, 2013, via Skype.

CHRISTINE: In "The Teacher/Scholar: Reconstructing Our Professional Identity in Two-Year Colleges," Jeff Andelora noted that most community college faculty tend to identify first as teachers of English in a two-year college rather than identifying as a disciplinary identity within rhetoric or composition or literature. Where do you see yourself and, by extension, your writing?

HOWARD: Well, that's an excellent question. [laughs] That's one I've thought on for a long time. I think that's an accurate assessment about two-year college folk, because they're generalists and teach both comp[osition] and literature; they see themselves somewhat more like English faculty rather than composition and rhetoric faculty. And we have some creative writers as well or people who have MFAs or Masters of Creative Writing who might see themselves as somewhat set apart from comp rhet[oric]. Truth be told, a good deal

DOI: 10.7330/9781607326625.c012

of the comp teaching at two-year colleges is taught by a contingent faculty, indeed, so full-time faculty tend to gravitate towards some of the lit classes. We have a two semester requirement. First semester is expository writing and second semester is kind of writing about literature, and many of the full-time faculty gravitate toward that second course for all kinds of obvious reasons. As for myself, I'm a comp rhet person. I teach mostly the writing 101 with some British literature survey but I'm pretty much a comp guy.

CHRISTINE: **Another finding that was mentioned in the *Cs* [College Composition and Communication] essay I referred to was that two-year college faculty who publish tend to draw on a wide variety of disciplines to support their research, such as education and psychology. They don't worry as much about disciplinary loyalties in their scholarship. Do you also draw from a larger pool of research even though you identify as a composition specialist as a scholar?**

HOWARD: That was certainly the case when I was involved in a writing center. I directed a writing center for many years, and I worked with faculty from across various disciplines. It was really wonderful work and the writing in the disciplines work was delightful. That interdisciplinary focus certainly influenced my own research. Despite the broad reach of some of the work, I think that community college faculty tend to be more insular than perhaps other folks, and given the time constraints and the labor-intensive work, I suspect that we don't get out all that much . . . [laughs]

CHRISTINE: **[laughs] I see.**

HOWARD: . . . and so we kind of stay within our own department or division. We do have divisional setups in many community colleges so we may be hanging around in meetings with people from the arts area, for example, theater certainly and communications, but not necessarily psychology or history. I happen to teach an interdisciplinary Holocaust course with a colleague in history, and that's a great experience, but I don't think it happens often enough at the community college. The local and specific nature of the community college setting has definitely influenced what I want to write about.

CHRISTINE: **Some of my MA students have finished reading your co-authored *Community College Writer* monograph and we discussed the opening narratives in this text. In one of your narratives you mention how doing a lot of "talk" about scholarly matters, publishing, or presenting at conferences is sometimes considered suspect among some of your colleagues, or maybe even elitist, perhaps because it is away from the "on the ground" work of the two-year college. And then, at the same time, you regularly publish, you maintain an active professional presence, you've chaired the Cs conference. How do you create an academic writing environment at Bristol Community College for yourself knowing that some of these suspicions about scholarly work exist?**

HOWARD: That's also a very good question. And it's a struggle, to be honest with you. I do have colleagues very close to me who are similarly engaged in scholarly writing. As I mentioned I team teach a course with someone from history, and I've got some folks who read the journals and who are doing some really good classroom research and writing about it. For example, J. P. Nadeau, with whom I authored that book, is a close colleague and we exchange ideas a great deal and have presented together. I try to make it a personal mission of mine to bring as many colleagues as I can to Cs and try to get them into the conversation! [laughs]

CHRISTINE: Bringing newcomers to the 4Cs might help break down perceptions that more global, scholarly work out there isn't relevant to a local context like a community college in a specific area of the country reaching a specific population.

HOWARD: I hope it helps. I do try to serve as a scholarly mentor as much as I possibly can, but again, to be perfectly honest, it's a struggle to maintain the kind of scholarly interactions within the field and while obviously teaching many classes and being part of the community college experience. Both the global and local sides take a large amount of time.

CHRISTINE: Yet despite the heavy teaching load, you have managed to find time to both serve the larger field of rhetoric and composition and publish. Can you tell us a little bit about some of your personal writing habits? How do you actually go about writing for publication in the community college environment?

HOWARD: Well, I'm a morning person so I do a lot of my writing in the morning and some of my reading in the afternoon. Most of the heavy writing is done in the summers, and when the weather's nice I'll be outside in the backyard with my laptop and working there. Whenever I find the time to write, I tend not to write in long stretches but rather in more of an episodic way. Still, when I get into a flow I can also do that pretty well and I enjoy that experience if I have enough time available.

CHRISTINE: It sounds like academic writing comes fairly easily for you?

HOWARD: Just the opposite. As I say to my students, writing has never come easily for me so it can be a bit of struggle to get the meaning out and onto the screen, and I certainly have to revise a great deal.

CHRISTINE: Has your academic writing process changed at all over the years even if it hasn't necessarily gotten easier?

HOWARD: I have found that over the years I'm doing fewer drafts. I seem to be clearer in what I need to say. I'm also more willing to share my work, believe it or not, with colleagues at certain crucial moments. When I first started out I was pretty much on my own trying to get things together, and the writing showed it. I'm a firm believer in peer review to make my writing stronger. I try make that case with colleagues as well.

CHRISTINE: Does sharing your writing prior to publication help get it closer to a finished product?

HOWARD: Yes. And it's so much easier now to share writing now electronically and digitally than it used to be. Like my students, when I get my feedback I want to read comments very closely and not get too anxious, but there is some affective component here and I'm as defensive as the next person about the kind of feedback I might get. I know I am a better writer when I share my writing with colleagues though.

CHRISTINE: Do you share your writing process with students in your classroom?

HOWARD: I don't do that as much as I used to and I'd certainly like to do more. My pedagogy has changed so much over the years. I teach the 101s and I'm currently in a new communication lab that we've set up—interesting modules, nicely configured round tables, portable tables. We move around a lot and now I'm just trying to figure out the dynamics of the set up. I haven't gone back to bringing my own writing back into it yet, but certainly I reference it a great deal.

CHRISTINE: You wrote in the *Community College Writer* that the most intense conversation about writing continues to take place in the required writing courses. You have a deep commitment to bring students' voices into their writing. Are you able to use your own writing practices to encourage students to reflect on how they write?

HOWARD: Sometimes. When so much emphasis is being placed on job readiness, career readiness, it's important for students to see real-world connections that writing can provide, and I try to make those connections. Especially when you consider that students are learning writing within the larger context of the threatened humanities. Helping students find their voices is always a challenge, but particularly so at the two-year college.

CHRISTINE: Knowing these conditions firsthand, is it important to you to use student voices in your own writing?

HOWARD: Absolutely. In fact, I had a conversation with J. P. Nadeau, the colleague I mentioned before, about my chair's address for Cs. I asked his advice and he said, "Well, do what you normally do which is to provide cases and draw from personal experience of students. Recreate their voices and bring their own writing into the address." I'm taking him at heart here and that is indeed what I'm doing as I draft it. That's always been a special pleasure of mine—to be able to work with student writing, to be able to offer it as a really good source of research, to be able to collaborate with students in trying to present or reconstruct the reality of the community college classroom.

CHRISTINE: This seems like a unique structure for a Cs chair's address since many of those addresses seem to focus on global issues in the field of rhetoric and composition as the field continues to develop as a discipline.

HOWARD: It makes my presentation somewhat more varied, because it's not just my voice but other voices as well. And I'm fully mindful, and I've been taught by many folks in our discipline, that I need to be careful with how I construct the students in my work. I want to make certain that they're okay with my representation and I've done a fairly decent job. Research based in the classroom has obviously been a career long part of my agenda.

CHRISTINE: I did an interview with Joe Harris a while back and we talked a lot about representation of student voices and how in the past there were no real protocols, but now rhetoric and composition researchers want to represent the student experience fairly and carefully to give contributors to our research a voice.

HOWARD: I was just thinking about that as I was preparing a draft of my address. I was going over some comment that a student had sent to me as part of an interview that we had done and I had some questions about it. The comment didn't seem as logical as I thought it should have been or provide as much factual material. Instead of letting it go, I did some searching around to determine whether the facts as the student knew them were true and found a conflict. This answer from her interview was about her own country—she's an immigrant—and so I will now go back to her and confirm what the facts are. So, it's not enough just to quote these students or even to rely on their own memories of what their lives were back in the old world, but we also have the responsibility to go back to try to do some research to give student testimony some context and validity.

CHRISTINE: As we've been talking about the chair's address for the 4Cs conference, I want to ask you about another claim that Cs about the two-year college article mentioned. The author noted that a lot of the two-year college folks who are involved in the field of writing do attend the 4Cs conference but nobody is really looking to that space as their key place of identification. Instead these two-year writing faculty tend to identify more with the TYCA (Two Year College English Association) conference. You probably are aware of this lack of identification for community college faculty with the Cs as you write your chair's address. Were you able to bring in some of those concerns for two-year faculty who don't feel represented?

HOWARD: I hope to do that. But I've been mindful since I became chair that I need to somehow cast my net broadly beyond the two-year college and look at the whole of it, the totality of the discipline, the various challenges that we face. But I am who I am. I teach at a public community college and that was clear in my call for program proposals and it will be clear in my chair's address too.

CHRISTINE: I realize you are very busy with duties as chair of the 4Cs. When you get some time, what's the next writing project you would like to take up?

HOWARD: Well, assuming as I rotate through the officers' service that I'll have a little more time to do these things, I'm thinking about working more with the writing of veterans. I've had more and more experience working with student vets in my classroom and I've been doing a little bit of reading about that work. That's one area I might explore. I've also been thinking over the years of writing a kind of teaching memoir. Anything's possible. We'll see how it goes.

CHRISTINE: Were you thinking of a bigger project like a book or a smaller project like an article or a chapter in an edited collection?

HOWARD: In terms of the vet piece, probably starting as an article. I would conduct the research by sitting down with some vets and interviewing them. I'm really, as you probably know, interested in ethnographic work; the kind of qualitative research that has a human face and voice.

CHRISTINE: And the teaching memoir?

HOWARD: The teaching memoir? Who knows? It could be a longer project. I think being a teaching scholar at a community college is an interesting place to be and there is so much to write about. Let's just say one has to know the nuances. It's been a career-long concern of mine that when writing faculty come to the community college they continue to be part of not only that community, but this larger disciplinary community whether regional or national, and they continue to read and write and continue to learn. And that's crucial.

13

THOMAS RICKERT

THOMAS RICKERT is professor in the English Department at Purdue University. His areas of interest include histories and theories of rhetoric, critical theory, composition, cultural studies, and network culture. His first book, *Acts of Enjoyment*, won the Gary Olson Award for best book in rhetoric and cultural studies in 2007. His second book, *Ambient Rhetoric: The Attunements of Rhetorical Being*, won the Gary Olson Award for best book in rhetoric and cultural studies in 2014, and it also won the Outstanding Monograph of the Year Award for 2014 from the Conference on College Communication and Composition. He has also composed multimedia work, his most recent being "Ambient Composition: Exteriorizing Donald Murray's 'The Interior View'" in *Enculturation*. His current book project explores a prehistory of rhetoric, with two essays from the project published so far: "Parmenides, Ontological Enaction, and the Prehistory of Rhetoric" in *Philosophy and Rhetoric* and "Rhetorical Prehistory and the Paleolithic" in *Review of Communication*.

Besides his scholarly work, Rickert teaches graduate and undergraduate classes in rhetorical theory in Purdue's Rhetoric and Composition program. He also regularly mentors new instructors for teaching first-year composition. Rickert has received two Fellowships in the Humanities at Purdue. He serves on the editorial board of the journal *Enculturation* and is a co-editor for the Lauer Series in Rhetoric and Composition (Parlor Press) and the RSA Series in Transdisciplinary Rhetoric (Penn State University Press). Rickert's interview took place on September 13, 2013, via Skype.

CHRISTINE: When I interviewed Jonathan Alexander for this project, he mentioned your name as a faculty writer in the field of rhetoric and composition he admired. When I asked him why, he noted that you manage to write theoretically deep pieces but at the same time have clear writing. Are there any deliberate writing moves that you use to balance difficult concepts with readable prose?

DOI: 10.7330/9781607326625.c013

THOMAS: Let me say that Jonathan is a very fine individual! [laughs] When you first learn to do theory as a grad student, you can fall in love with the language of theory and its density and ambiguity. After a while you get to a point where you realize you want to be more accessible, and that density and ambiguity can just be a part of the whole repertoire of moves you are trying to bring to what you are trying to say. I have gravitated more towards trying to think through my theory more concretely.

CHRISTINE: Can you explain how this practice works in your writing?

THOMAS: When I write, I think theory through by finding an image or an example that allows the theory to show up in a way that is graspable. I want to connect with the reader.

CHRISTINE: Do you apply this writing style to both print and multimodal pieces or does your composing process differ? You compose in both venues for scholarly publication and there would be different spaces to illustrate difficult concepts.

THOMAS: A lot of my invention takes place via externalization where I work out what I want to say and how I want to say it. For example, reading things, looking at things, creating comparisons there. So when I do more multimedia work, I look at a lot of stuff and go to a lot of websites, so there is a lot of browsing involved. I want to find just the right image, or just the right link, or just the right sound to illustrate a concept. That invention or discovery process is a little bit different from more print based materials. But not that different because I am still looking at lots of books or essays to find my way.

CHRISTINE: Do you prefer composing in one medium over the other?

THOMAS: Multimedia composing is more fun . . . but not less rigorous. There is just something about trying to assemble different strands of different levels of meaning beyond print. It's a lot of fun and I'm often surprised with the results. It does take a lot of time.

CHRISTINE: What do you do to manage your time? How do you find time to write?

THOMAS: You write when you can and you use deadlines to help you. And there is something I describe as "academic triage." If it's going to die out there no matter what, it's going to die out there no matter what. An essay just won't get finished because it's something you can't complete in the time you have or you aren't really interested in that particular writing project anymore. And the writing you bring into focus is the stuff you know is going to survive as long as you get to it right then. I think most of us who are really busy use something like that academic triage. I use it because I have three kids. [laughs]

CHRISTINE: Jessica Enoch and I discussed in her interview how having kids helps parents to manage time since there is no choice but to be organized. You don't really sit there and debate about writing; you just go and write, because that's the time that is available to you.

THOMAS: Right, and you are more aware of time. I try to use conferences and presentations to help me get focused and writing. I also had to learn to write at night and to revise at night. I find that caffeine and alcohol are very helpful.

CHRISTINE: Where do you like to write?

THOMAS: I find that where I am writing matters a lot to me. I don't know if this showed up as an issue for the other people that you interviewed but place is important. I do a great deal of writing outside the home. I write a lot in coffee shops.

CHRISTINE: Place is mentioned frequently with about half of the folks needing to write before going into work so they aren't distracted and the others needing to write at work so they aren't distracted. Why is it that coffee shops work for you?

THOMAS: Home has too many distractions. Especially for drafting, I like writing in a coffee shop. I like taking the books I need there to work for a few hours for concentrated writing. Within the coffee shop there is a certain amount of hubbub but it is not too much. It is enough that it asks me to concentrate in a certain way and it helps me to focus on precisely whatever it is that I have set out for myself to do that day. Or for that hour or two or three or whatever it is that I have. I find that the slight hubbub helps me focus and the amount of work is just right for that moment. Plus, there is the caffeine . . . [laughs]

CHRISTINE: Do you have a backup plan for writing if you can't get to the coffee shop? For example, if you only have an hour between classes for revising an essay?

THOMAS: Yes, the coffee shop is great for drafting, but I can revise at home in the evening. I have a hard time drafting late at night because I am too tired, but I can revise. I put a little music on, have a little glass of wine, and work. When I was doing the *Ambient Rhetoric* book, I would write for about four hours in the morning at a local coffee shop and I would come home. This was during the summer when I had no teaching duties. After lunch, I would go in the basement where I have a very nice stereo with a ton of vinyl records and I would play a lot of ambient, German electronic or jazz stereo. I would write for another two or three hours.

CHRISTINE: Most writing faculty would be jealous of that large span of time to work on the book!

THOMAS: That was probably how the book on ambience got done. That was the only time that I was able to write at home drafting.

CHRISTINE: You talk about sound quite a bit in your work. Is using music part of your composing process or does it affect how you write? Is there a mental connection between how you listen to music and how you write?

THOMAS: One of the things that made me start of thinking about the issue of ambiance was music, and it did impact my composing, especially because I realized there are certain kinds of music I can write to and there are certain kinds that I can't. Mellower jazz and a lot of electronic is just perfect for writing. A beat can be structured with more psychedelic or free-forming music over the top that is not melody based. I love how the structured and unstructured work together. The underlying beat works as a sort of structure and the free-flowing music over the top goes with the flow of the mind and, similarly for me, the words on the page.

CHRISTINE: It is interesting to hear how you see the connection.

THOMAS: Music can just dominate a space. But I think it also matters for how I compose.

CHRISTINE: It sounds like you are using music to write when you are alone, yet you have done a fair bit of collaboration with others on both print and multimodal pieces. How do you navigate that collaborative writing process?

THOMAS: [laughs] I have found that maybe there is some commonality in collaboration, but in a lot of ways, every time that I write with someone else it is a new thing. You have to sort out who is going to do what sorts of work. And it's not clear cut as in, "I am going to handle this section" and "you are going to handle that section." Because at least in the writing that I have done that's collaborative, we get into each other's sections almost immediately. Somebody may be the main drafter but the other person's voice may come through, and collaborators have to find some balance. I have found that to get to that balance you have to do about at least a quarter to a half more work than if you were writing alone. People think that collaborative writing is easier. It takes up less time but really you make up the time that you might think you would save with the extra work in figuring out how to negotiate the writing process with the other person.

CHRISTINE: But collaborative writing is still important to you.

THOMAS: Yes, it is rewarding because often times that other person will have a body of knowledge that you don't have. At the same time an essay is never just about the body of knowledge that you have; it is about finding an angle in that body of knowledge and making an argument. And so writing with another person entails getting in their head space in a certain way. It takes a certain letting go of yourself so that you can think in the way that they think and so really get what it is that they are trying to do on the page.

CHRISTINE: How do you exchange the writing then, when you write with someone else? Do you exchange over email or do you physically get together and talk it out first?

THOMAS: I usually trade drafts back and forth, and when I wrote with my wife, Jenny [Bay], we did it mainly through trading drafts back and forth even though we are in the same house and could actually talk to each other. It sped the writing up in a lot of ways and got the work published more quickly.

CHRISTINE: **I'm also part of an academic couple and so is Cheryl Glenn who I am interviewing later this week. Do you and Jenny write near each other or together? For example, when you go out on your coffee shop writing date, does she bring her laptop and plug away too so you have some company?**

THOMAS: We have done that a little bit, but more and more we have gravitated towards carving out our own space. We do talk a lot, but in terms of the actual drafting, not so much. Then again, we do have the opportunity to read each other's writing all the time and so we send each other our drafts or our hard copies. We read them and give each other feedback all the time so we have that advantage. That happens a lot.

CHRISTINE: **In terms of your own writing processes, do you make a deliberate attempt to convey any of these practices we've talked about to your students?**

THOMAS: I try to. In fact, I was talking with my mentor group about this today. The most inventive material you will ever come up with comes from working with revising a draft. Typically, my greatest insights will come from that and forcing me to go back and do various forms of revision, but it always comes from working out a problem that I wasn't aware was a problem yet.

CHRISTINE: **Does this advice also happen in, say, a graduate level course or in a more structured teaching environment?**

THOMAS: Yes. I am teaching a review writing course right now. I actually do a lot of reviewing and writing book reviews. And so I just tell students the things I struggle with as a reviewer. I also tell them about the limitations that I am under when writing for an academic audience. For example, I don't feel that I can be nearly as stylish as I would like to be.

CHRISTINE: **Stylish academic writing is difficult to come by. I know some researchers such as Helen Sword are trying to study why academics like to read stylish academic writing but struggle to write it.**

THOMAS: Style is one of the reasons that in my writing I try to slip in all kinds of things that are really subtle or that I find funny or interesting or enjoyable. For example, I like to put in a ton of music allusions in my writing.

CHRISTINE: **Maybe that's why Jonathan admires your writing style!**

THOMAS: Maybe he picks up on it. You can get away with more of that in the public realm, but I think you can still do it in academia, and it helps to make your writing fresh and interesting. I put in several Led Zeppelin references in the introduction to my book as a way to make a point I needed to make.

CHRISTINE: **We recently had Ellen Bauerle from University of Michigan Press talk to our graduate students about successful academic writing. She told them that just because they need to make academic argu-**

ments as authors, it doesn't preclude them from writing in an interesting or stylish way. Stylish writing stands out to editors.

THOMAS: It's good advice. I think that being interesting will help you at any level as long as you have other things going with it. As a writer, you just can't just be interesting, obviously. I mean, the thinking has to be sound; the research has to be good.

CHRISTINE: I edit the Praxis section for *Kairos* right now and I see this struggle all the time. We often have someone write a piece where they do a lot of interesting things with the media and even compose the webtext in an interesting writing style, but after we dig deeper we realize the piece is not really making an argument, or at least not a very clear one.

THOMAS: Right. At the same time, I am very much interested in what people use as touchstones in their writing since these touchstones also lend style to an essay. There are a good number of people even in the field who like to talk about classical music or they like to talk about Shakespeare and literary culture. I have made a deliberate attempt to try to make a different matrix of allusions keyed to rock music and popular culture.

CHRISTINE: So deliberately going anti-canon in a way?

THOMAS: Or just offering a new canon. That's my culture, that's my music and what I grew up with and I think it is important. I think that Bob Dylan is important or Neil Young or whoever. So I like building in allusions to that type of music because it reinforces the fact that that stuff matters to some of us and that it is part of who we are.

CHRISTINE: I am hoping after these interviews are published, someone can go back to your work and look for those musical references and will understand why they are happening because they have the "back story." It's part of a deliberate attempt to make the academic writing interesting to you but also stylish for the reader.

THOMAS: Thank you. Talking about my writing was a lot of fun and I can't wait to read the whole thing. I think this is going to be a smashing project.

14
JACQUELINE ROYSTER

JACQUELINE JONES ROYSTER is the dean of Georgia Tech's Ivan Allen College of Liberal Arts. She holds the Ivan Allen Jr. dean's chair in Liberal Arts and Technology and is professor of English in the School of Literature, Media, and Communication. Royster has authored three books: *Southern Horrors and Other Writings: The Anti-Lynching Campaign of Ida B. Wells-Barnett, Traces of a Stream: Literacy and Social Change among African American Women,* and *Profiles of Ohio Women, 1803–2003.* She co-authored *Feminist Rhetorical Studies: New Horizons in Rhetoric, Composition, and Literacy Studies.* Her research centers on rhetorical studies, literacy studies, and women's studies, areas in which she has authored and co-authored numerous articles and book chapters as well as several co-edited works.

With regard to teaching, Royster has taught writing and writing related courses across all levels of the curriculum. Likewise, with administrative leadership, she has served in multiple capacities. In 1978 she was the founder of the Comprehensive Writing Program and the Writing Center at Spelman College; the director of the Writing Program and the vice chair for Rhetoric and Composition at The Ohio State University. Royster has served as both chair and secretary of the Conference on College Composition and Communication (CCCC). She has received two of 4C's highest honors: The Exemplar Award for excellence in research, leadership, and service and the Braddock Award for the best article in *College Composition and Communication.* Royster also received the Modern Language Association's Mina P. Shaughnessy Prize for the best book in the teaching of English and the Frances A. March Award for distinguished service to the profession. In 2000 the state of Ohio named her a Pioneer in Higher Education due to her professional record. The interview took place on February 27, 2014, via Skype.

CHRISTINE: In doing research for this collection, I've found that administrative work takes a toll on writing faculty more heavily than on faculty

DOI: 10.7330/9781607326625.c014

in other areas. In your career, you've held some specifically discipline based administrative positions such as the writing program administrator and writing center director, and now you are serving as the Dean of the College of Liberal Arts. Through all of these positions you've managed to publish regularly. How do you find the time to write?

JACKIE: Well, I think that part of finding the time is having the passion and will. And what was always clear to me as a human being is that I would not be happy as an academic if I could not find a way to do my own work. With the jobs I chose to accept, what that meant over the years was that I had to have the commitment to finding the time and trying, to the extent I could, of maintaining a space and time for doing my own work. Now I will say it's a constant challenge.

CHRISTINE: How so, specifically?

JACKIE: Looking back, what I realize is that at some points in my life, making time to write meant not getting enough sleep and not spending the amount of time with my family that I wanted to spend. I had to really struggle to balance out wanting to do my work with other responsibilities in a satisfying way. I'm still trying to balance the need for doing my own work with what has to be done in a given day for my administrative position while also considering the needs of my family.

CHRISTINE: Because you are juggling a lot of responsibilities, are there any writing techniques that really work for you?

JACKIE: Yes! Developing a habit of quick focusing and getting to work immediately as soon as time opens up. If I've got one morning, I have to find a way to quick focus. If I've got a day on a weekend, I have to find a way to quick focus so I'm so intently focused on what I'm doing that I try to make whatever progress I can make. The other strategy that has worked for me is just figuring out how to combine priorities. For example, if I take an invitation to give a talk, I try to craft that talk so that it helps me to think about whatever it is that I'm working on and get mutual feedback from the people to whom I'm presenting.

CHRISTINE: When you have a small pocket of time open in your day, how do you know where to start? Do you say, have a list of three things you want to work on and, you know, just go right to the list and start or is there some other way you get yourself ready to work or in focus, as you describe?

JACKIE: Well, I don't know if I have a systematic habit of coming to focus, but I do have a habit I use to get organized, and I think I've written about it actually. I do have a habit of organizing myself in file folders. And at one point, I even had a color-coded kind of system of putting things in different colors so that it signaled to me that these folders had some priority in the day's work. That was one system of just trying to keep everything together in one place that allows me to quickly go to that place and see where I was the last time I looked. I can pick right up where I left off and start working again.

CHRISTINE: I see. Are you still using that system or was it something you used while on the tenure track?

JACKIE: I used that system for a time when I was more committed to multi-tasking. [laughs]

CHRISTINE: [laughs]

JACKIE: As all my folders tend to look alike and I have so many piles now in my current position that I have to have a system for my system! [both laugh]

CHRISTINE: I imagine you do!

JACKIE: But at one point, having a color-coded file system was really a kind of a focusing strategy. I've found that as you change positions you often need to adjust your system to respond to your current life. For example, when I had small children, it was getting my family to understand that if you can give Mommy an hour here then I'll give you an hour there. When I could close the door and work for a short bit of time uninterrupted, I could then give my family undivided attention.

CHRISTINE: Balancing family and work life is a clear theme emerging from these interviews. Is there anything else difficult for you about the writing process besides finding the time?

JACKIE: I've always made the case that the difficult part about writing is not the writing, it's the thinking. You know, getting myself to the point where I feel that I'm thinking well, coherently, and consistently about whatever the topic of concern is the challenge. I want to *feel* that I'm in focus. I can try to get myself in focus but the real challenge is *feeling* in focus. "Oh yeah, this is where I want to be with this idea. I like this sentence. Oh right, this is a good article that I want to keep in scope or this is the thought that I want to carry from this part to that part." So it's the thinking part. The writing for me has always been a moment of joy.

CHRISTINE: I think you've just put into words what many faculty both inside and outside the discipline are feeling. In many of these interviews, writing faculty clearly like to write, but having your head in the right place to be able to do it is often tough with the schedules we keep.

JACKIE: I can get passionate about writing projects and that passion helps me stay in focus. I'm always thinking about the subject, even when I'm not working, because I'm engaged with the topic.

CHRISTINE: Much of your work focuses on African-American rhetoric and writing and, more specifically, feminist issues. Does your subject matter affect how you write in any way?

JACKIE: Yes, though it's not exclusively African-American women and feminist projects but it's certainly defined by that perspective. I try to be true to writing from my own identity location, my own value location.

CHRISTINE: How does your value location affect your writing?

JACKIE: I am passionate about my subject matter. I care about the women I study. I care about supporting more visibility for the quality of the work they have done in the world, so in that way, yes, there is a connection between the subject matter and the rhetorical subjects that I'm looking at; the rhetorical context that I'm looking at.

CHRISTINE: And when writing about other subjects?

JACKIE: I have to say that I have multiple passions that influence my writing, and I get pretty passionate about writing about students. I'm a pretty human-centered kind of person so I have to care about the thing that I'm writing about in order to feel like I'm in that focused zone that I was talking about a few minutes ago.

CHRISTINE: You mentioned students. Does your writing influence your teaching and the types of strategies you advocate in your textbook authorship? I know that's kind of a different animal from the projects we've been discussing, but maybe not. [laughs]

JACKIE: [laughs] It's not, really. I've always been committed in the way that I've taught writing and I have to say that I haven't taught it consistently for a long time because my commitment to these higher level administrative positions made me conclude that I could not give the kind of time and attention to a writing course that I felt that my students in those courses deserved, so I just refused to do it. I did not want to shortchange my students. The writing courses call for a level of time and attention that I could not give, because the students are kind of "in the making" in the way that my graduate students were not.

CHRISTINE: These courses are definitely time intensive due to the commenting and conferencing.

JACKIE: And that's why I did not teach a writing course for almost ten years. While the world of teaching writing courses has changed dramatically, by the way, I should say.

CHRISTINE: [laughs] It has!

JACKIE: I did teach when I left Ohio State, but I chose to teach the second level writing course, which was my favorite course. At that point I was not doing any administration and I had loads of fun. So the writing assignments that I've developed over the years were based on two principles: one, I would not ask students to write about anything I didn't want to read.

CHRISTINE: [laughs]

JACKIE: And two, I would not ask students to write anything that I had not tried to write myself.

CHRISTINE: I suspect this is not the case for other textbook authors. But what a great way to test out how an assignment feels.

JACKIE: I wanted to feel the "on the ground" response to the assignments. The only way I could get that feeling was doing them myself.

CHRISTINE: Were the students aware that you were also writing these assignments yourself? They know that you had also tried them?

JACKIE: Sometimes they did, and sometimes they didn't. That was a kind of an ethical commitment that I made regardless of whether I shared my process for developing the textbook with students or not. But doing the actual assignments myself often helped when addressing the questions that they were asking me about particular assignments, because I always asked them to ask liberally questions about their concerns about a particular task or particular assignment. The responses that I gave to students in response to these questions demonstrated that I had tried [each assignment] out.

CHRISTINE: I imagine these responses also lent some credibility to you as the instructor. Did doing the assignments help you with your own writing?

JACKIE: Yes, doing the assignments helped me clarify how I was framing the assignments in the textbook but also I feel any practice writing is useful on some level.

CHRISTINE: You've written a lot of significant pieces for the field of rhetoric and composition as well as some interdisciplinary work. When you think back on your whole career, what writing piece are you most proud of?

JACKIE: It's difficult to choose, because one of the things that I'm most proud of as a writer, or I should say the *thing* I'm most proud of, is my body of work because I believe that body of work has come out of my passion for the things that I wanted to know. My work shows how I was willing to engage seriously in trying to know what I was learning, and striving to convey that in a compelling way to others. But the project that remains, my *heart* project and soul project, as I have described it before, is *Traces of a Stream.*

CHRISTINE: Was there something different about the writing process with that particular project that just stands out to you?

JACKIE: I don't know if it's the process that is different. I think the process is probably the same because I am passionate about a lot of projects. But that project stands out to me for a particular reason. A lot of people don't know how long it took me to do that book!

CHRISTINE: [laughs]

JACKIE: [laughs] It took me a good fifteen years to do that book. And it evolved. There were times when I thought it was ready and I could've gotten some kind of publication out, and essentially I've described what the women I researched told me, "Uh-uh! Not yet."

CHRISTINE: [laughs] What about this project took so much time?

JACKIE: [laughs] I had to get the writing right. And so I had to keep working on it. Because when I write I have to try and to know *well* what I am trying to know; that took time with this project especially.

It took time because I was trying to communicate well what I had learned about the women I was researching.

CHRISTINE: Would you say that because you cared so much about the subject matter you weren't sure when the project was finished? Or was it because you kept finding more to write about? Or were you fussing with revisions?

JACKIE: A little bit of all of these because this project reveals who I am as a writer and, by association, the passion and dedication I have when I write. That project remains for me my soul project. There are other projects I am proud of, but *Traces of a Stream* captures so much of my passion for writing and research.

15
KRISTINE BLAIR

KRISTINE L. BLAIR is professor of English and dean of the College of Liberal Arts and Social Sciences at Youngstown State University. The author or co-author of numerous publications on gender and technology, the politics of distance learning, electronic portfolios, and feminist pedagogies, Blair currently serves as editor of both the international print journal *Computers and Composition* and its separate companion journal *Computers and Composition Online*. She is also a recipient of the Conference on College Composition and Communication's Technology Innovator Award and the Computers and Composition Charles Moran Award for Distinguished Contributions to the Field.

A former member of the doctoral program in Rhetoric and Writing at Bowling Green State University (BGSU) from 1996 to 2016, where she also served as Department Chair from 2005 to 2014, Blair's career as a writing teacher has been a diverse one. Early in her career she taught in California community college programs that included Folsom Prison. She has also developed and taught computer literacy courses for older adults in Wood County, Ohio and developed and co-facilitated the Digital Mirror Computer Camp for Girls, a federally funded initiative for which she received BGSU's President's Award for Collaborative Research with Graduate Students. As a graduate educator, Blair has directed over fifty dissertations and served as the chair of the CCCC Consortium of Doctoral Programs in Rhetoric and Composition. She received BGSU Graduate Student Senate's Outstanding Contributor to Graduate Education Award in 2004 and 2009, along with a doctoral advisee award for her supervision of BGSU's award-winning dissertation in the Humanities in 2015. A former faculty Senate Chair, in 2014 Blair received BGSU's Women of Distinction Award as well as the BGSU Faculty Senate Award for Leadership as a Department Chair. Blair's interview took place on July 15, 2013, in Christine Tulley's office at The University of Findlay.

DOI: 10.7330/9781607326625.c015

CHRISTINE: You have several projects where work is explicitly feminist: articles, book chapters, edited collections, while other projects are less so. Has your methodology changed over the years?

KRIS: I think that I've gone from a strictly theoretical frame, in terms of feminist theory and method, to much more of an action oriented frame. The emphasis may be different in the pieces I write but the goals might be similar. It's not all that different from when you and I started work back in 1999 researching cybergirls and working with adolescent girls' literacy practices.

CHRISTINE: How do you think you've moved from theory to action in your writing?

KRIS: I think the difference from moving from theory to action is that I started branching out and working with different populations. We worked with adolescent girls. I've worked with senior citizens. I've worked with faculty. I've certainly worked again with adolescent girls for a more recent camp at BGSU. I've written about all of these projects. So it's about finding those contexts to write about and working from there versus starting with theory first.

CHRISTINE: Does the writing itself start differently?

KRIS: A lot of the writing that I initially end up doing starts as something like grant writing so you can get the resources to carry out some of these different multimodal research methods, whether feminist or not. That research is used to tell the later stories in the articles or chapters.

CHRISTINE: Would you say your work is becoming more narrative in nature?

KRIS: I think narrative has always been part of it, even from the very beginning. In the research on literacy of older adults, I developed a curriculum, taught a class for senior citizens, collected data based on the findings, and really figured out the best way to both collect and represent that data. I'm very interested in, and have always been interested in, the role of narrative as a form of methodology, and I don't think that's changed so much. I think that the different contexts in which my narrative and feminist interests have played out over the years have changed. I'm also more interested in viewing the populations I research as not necessarily participants or subjects in the really clinical, objective sense but as partners I find.

CHRISTINE: Can you explain what you mean by that?

KRIS: I think as I research and write it means finding people who teach you as much as you teach them *and* involving them as co-researchers, co-learners, co-authors. I've tried to do more of that in my work over the years. Sometimes it doesn't always manifest itself in the ways that it does for some people like Cindy [Selfe] and Gail [Hawisher] where some of their participants become co-authors on pieces, but it's about finding a way to represent their voices. What better way to do that than allowing them to speak on the page or speak on the screen and theorize their experience?

CHRISTINE: You also co-author a lot of pieces. How do you feel about collaboration as part of the feminist enterprise?

KRIS: I think it's important to find ways to write co-equally with graduate students in particular. That's such a crucial part of what we should do when directing a graduate program. When you create these opportunities, you recognize that in some ways the graduate students who help you transcribe are authors too because they're the ones who are making some of those selections about getting rid of the "uhs" and the "ahs" that affect a final publication.

CHRISTINE: It sounds like you try to set up a different co-authoring relationship from the start.

KRIS: Yes. It's really important to figure out those dynamics and I think a deliberate effort to use feminist frameworks and feminist methods also helps to ensure tensions between graduate student writers and faculty are not swept under the rug when they co-author a piece.

CHRISTINE: As one of your co-authors, I know how much you value collaborative writing in your career. Because you co-author frequently, have these co-authored pieces helped influence your own writing process?

KRIS: I think that when you're talking about writing, part of the problem is that you can't only focus on the writing aspect. It's the research aspect as well. I think that the passion and the enthusiasm for the research that we've had in our writing projects has certainly trickled down and extends to the way I write with current graduate students that I've had the honor of writing with. Collaboration feeds my energy as a writer. This idea of ebb and flow, of sometimes knowing when you're the lead on something and it's your energy, and your research, and even sometimes your connections because of person X who's doing an edited collection and other times knowing a co-author is the lead and a piece is starting from her connection, yet she wants my voice a part of it. Working collaboratively allows you to set the parameters of your own participation based on a project and where it originates.

CHRISTINE: Is there an example where you think collaboration worked especially well?

KRIS: I just finished a co-editing project with my colleague Lee Nickoson for a guest-edited edition of *Feminist Teacher* on feminism and community engagement. There were those moments in the collaboration where we were both there working together, and then those moments in the collaboration when she took on a role because I was out of town and vice versa. Collaboration works when you know that you have each other's back. You always have my back when we collaborate! [laughs]

CHRISTINE: [laughs] And you have mine.

KRIS: Collaborations work well when both parties are invested. I think so much of successful academic publication is dependent on your own motivation and passion that you bring to the project as a whole, even if you are writing it with someone else.

CHRISTINE: Is there anything else you've learned about successful collaboration?

KRIS: Yes, and you and I have actually written about that. There are times even when one person is listed as, say, the lead author; it's always presumed to be co-equal, but I still work with co-authors to figure out who is listed first. From a feminist standpoint we know, "Hey, it's your turn," or "Hey, you're the one who's going up for promotion," or "You're the one who's applying for this position." Those types of shifts and ebbs and flows in terms of responsibility are what make a collaboration successful and flexible.

CHRISTINE: At one time you were serving as chair of the English Department, chair of Faculty Senate, while editing *Computer and Composition* and *Computers and Composition Online*, and you were still teaching. How did you find time to write?

KRIS: I think the difficulty of being an administrator is that so much of the time it's all day, every day that you're in a singular space caught up with the things that land on your desk so you just have to kind of look for those pockets of opportunity. It's a very serendipitous process. For me, that usually involves a lot of evening writing because those pockets don't always present themselves. On collaborative projects where I know that I owe you something by a certain time and I realize, "Hey, I have three hours from 1:00 to 4:00 and I'm just going to sit down at my desk." That obligation helps me to complete the writing. And I remember when we worked on the piece for *Stories that Speak to Us,* a lot of the work was written at my desk at work in open moments.

CHRISTINE: That project was a large amount of work with the transcriptions and edits.

KRIS: I did those during the summer sitting at my desk at work. The problem is when you're in those administrative roles, those writing opportunities don't always present themselves. I think part of the challenge is that if you really see yourself as a scholar, and as a writer, not writing is kind of the death knell for your self-esteem. I've literally said, "I'm not going to let them get in my way." I am going to write. I am not going to let people get in my way of getting my writing done. And I've kind of stuck to that. It sounds kind of agonistic and hostile but it is this battle that you wage with yourself really, but you project that tension and that anxiety onto the external barriers. The people who come into your office without an appointment, the unexpected meeting that you have to have, the new project that somebody wants to involve the department in, and you're like, "Really? Where are we going to come up with all the faculty to contribute?" It's about making that balance between being proactive about your own writing and balancing that with the reacting to the crap that lands on your desk every single day. So yeah, I have been successful at that. [laughs]

CHRISTINE: [laughs]

KRIS: Although some people will say to me, "How did you manage to do it?" and I respond, "I just never stopped writing." That's why I believe in those sorts of adages of "write a page a day," "don't procrastinate," and others, because I'm not a quick writer. I really do need time to think and write badly and then see how the little bad things I've written get better with each passing day. As I rework them or reshape them they ultimately become readable by the general public. [laughs] Or maybe not. [laughs]

CHRISTINE: You work in both print and multimodal environments and you seem to be able and you're able to jump back and forth between those. When you're starting a project in print, is it different from the way you would start it for a multimodal project?

KRIS: I think that it's not all that different for me and that's part of the challenge. Because I think scholars in the area of multimodality always talk about the notion of "born digital." And in some ways even print, or even alphabetic text is "born digital," but we don't think of it that way. I have something to put in multimodal form before I can actually get it there. Some of the time management things are a little bit different. For me, the hardest part is always the writing itself. So just making sure I have text to deal with and then getting that into basic digital form is my starting point and then I go from there. There is a real process of layering in multimodal projects that I don't think you have in print projects. But for me they still always start with some form of alphabetic text because you have to figure out what media assets are going to go along with those projects themselves.

CHRISTINE: Is there a piece that you've written over the whole body of your work that you now wish you could go back and now revise for any reason?

KRIS: I do have a piece that I wish that I could revise. It's a very obscure piece that I wrote with Angela Haas and it's a webtext. It was published in the journal *Rhizomes,* which is edited by my colleague Ellen Berry, and it's on cyber-feminism and women's voices. It talks about women's relationship to technology, and we really relied on the wonderful Davin Heckman. He did the majority of the tech work for the piece due to his work with e-literature. When you look at it today, it was published like a decade ago. It's such a good piece, but the technology, like the background, is black and the text is neon red. Some of the text is neon green and neon blue. Some of the audio that's associated with the text is real jumpy.

CHRISTINE: The quality is not what it could be.

KRIS: I wish Angela and I could go back and take that piece and redo it in a nice way. It's innovatively designed. It's really funky and edgy and artsy, but it's not very accessible as a result, and I think if it were a contemporary webtext it would get so much traffic if it were nicely designed. I love that piece. And Jackie Rose at Computers and Writing actually came up to me and said something like, "You know, I saw that piece you did, you know, about ten years ago in *Rhizome*. Do you still do any kind of digital work like that?" But I wish I could go back because I had to say, "I'm a little embarrassed. That was a long time ago!" [laughs]

CHRISTINE: [laughs] It doesn't hold up from a design standpoint in the way print pieces do?

KRIS: When looking at early pieces, even from innovative journals like *Kairos*, everything is pretty static and not very image laden. There isn't much visual-textual integration, and the role that audio and video and multimodality in general now play in our understanding of meaning making and rhetoricity wasn't there. That's part of the challenge for people writing in digital spaces: keeping up with the various types of tools. It isn't just about learning audio and video, learning Audacity, learning how to use a webcam, etcetera. It's about transcribing, and figuring out the best software that will do that so work is accessible.

CHRISTINE: What would you like to leave as your legacy as a writer or contribution to the field of writing?

KRIS: I've been very fortunate because I've taught in a doctoral program, so in some ways, for me, the legacy is an easy, natural one. It is all the people who have graduated, whose dissertations I've chaired, who have gone on to do all these great things as teachers, as writers, and as digital scholars in the field. It is that sense of knowing that there are people who are passionate to write about the same things that you are, and they're not just former graduate students. They're colleagues and they're friends that you have the opportunity to continue working with. They also keep the cycle going, particularly because my schedule is packed as an administrator. I'll say, "Oh, how can I possibly work on that?" And someone like you or another colleague says, "Come on! We can do it!" The legacy from the doctoral program is that research network of people who sustain me as a scholar.

CHRISTINE: This network idea circles back to your point of why collaborative writing is so important.

KRIS: I think the research network gets away from that whole notion of the writer alone in his or her garret, spurred on by some form of creative genius that is wholly individual and ultimately doesn't exist. I think that's just part of that myth that, admittedly, keeps faculty writers from moving forward because of the emphasis still on the single-authored monograph and what that has to look like and who has to publish it.

CHRISTINE: And the emphasis on the single-authored research paper in the college writing courses we teach.

KRIS: And the dissertation as a form of individual print scholarship. Even though the MLA [Modern Language Association] made this call for a more capacious sense of scholarship, it's still not happening widely. I want my legacy as a writer to model what networked writing looks like in a variety of print and multimodal spaces. I've had the opportunity to contribute to that network based on all the people I've worked with, from former graduate students to colleagues who are out there participating in the discourse community of the field. Making that collaborative writing network both visible and valued will be my legacy.

16

CARVING OUT A WRITING LIFE IN THE DISCIPLINE OF RHETORIC AND COMPOSITION

What We Can Learn from Writing Faculty

As a collective, the interviews appear to offer two contradictory insights about how writing faculty write. On one hand, successful writing faculty do adopt similar viewpoints toward academic writing and use shared writing techniques as described in the Introduction's "Patterns for Analysis." Interviewees approach the writing process with similar attitudes of acceptance toward the complexity of composing and joy toward building a writing project, and use strategies of thinking rhetorically, invention strategies that scaffold writing, and "quick focus" to efficiently make forward progress on projects in small writing times. On the other hand, though there are clear patterns in the way writing faculty approach writing for publication, the interviews also reveal there is also an incredible amount of diversity in the way faculty *follow* these broad patterns. For example, though faculty write in short segments during the day, the pace of writing differs as some compose rapidly in bursts when enchanted with a new idea (DeVoss, Yancey) and others make slow progress by writing a little each day (Blair, Enoch, Selfe). And though faculty may take the long view of the composing process and accept that writing needs an incubation period, they use that period much differently: such as, Rickert finds a better focus for a project using revision, Yancey switches to another project, Roen switches to another section within the project, and Harris walks his dogs and thinks about writing. These are very diverse snapshots of productive and satisfying lives in our discipline.

In 2012, Helen Sword surveyed a thousand academic writers from all disciplines and found that the most successful did not write in the same way: "There's not just one way to be productive. Books and articles on 'how to be a productive writer' tend to be very bossy. They give you all these hard and fast rules, like you must write an hour a day, every day, for instance. What I'm finding as I talk to people, though, is there is a wide variety in the writing habits and practices of successful academics"

DOI: 10.7330/9781607326625.c016

(Sword as quoted in Brown 2014). The finding that writing faculty *don't* vary a great deal in general attitudes and habits, yet adapt similar practices in widely diverse ways to local employment contexts, career stages, family circumstances, and individual preferences for writing, suggests our disciplinary hegemony *does* affect writing for academic publication within the discipline.

So, what can this assortment of interviews teach us about how rhetoric and composition faculty carve out rewarding writing lives and how our discipline affects how we write? One overarching message stands out: *writing faculty experience and practice writing as a process.* This may seem obvious and perhaps clichéd, as we "know" that writing has many phases such as prewriting and revision and that revision and editing are different processes. But as a field we have come a long way since Louise Phelps (1998) argued that the term "process" historically was subject to shallow definitions when rhetoric and composition was still defining itself as a discipline.

Conceptualizing writing as process on a deeper level, in the way writing faculty talk about it in this collection, recognizes writing as a complex, messy, and individualized process or series of processes subject to influences from historical context, identity, education, and more. This conception of writing as a process defines the modern discipline. In *Threshold Concepts,* a collection of beliefs and practices in the field of writing studies as defined by leading scholars in the field, Alder-Kassner and Wardle note that contributors recognized an overarching master "metaconcept" where all threshold concepts stem: writing is simultaneously "an activity" (i.e., a process or series of processes) and "a subject of study" (Adler-Kassner and Wardle 2015, xxvii). Though Alder-Kassner and Wardle rightly note that not everyone within our own field may agree that writing is a subject of study, the recognition that writing is a process threads through virtually all of the threshold concepts that follow.

This concept of writing as a process is one we frequently instill in students using the introductions of the composition textbooks we write. For example, in their 2017 *Writing about Writing* textbook, Elizabeth Wardle and Doug Downs argue: "Writing is a process. It takes time and practice. Writing things that are new to you, writing longer texts, and writing with new kinds of technology all take practice. And no matter how much you practice, what you write will never be perfect . . . There is no such thing as perfect writing; writing is not in the category of things that are perfectible" (Wardle and Downs 2017, 16). In *Writing Today,* Richard Johnson-Sheehan and Charles Paine advise students that writing is a complex activity that requires practice and learning:

> To do something well, you first needed to learn the *process* for doing it. Someone else, perhaps a teacher, coach, parent, or friend, showed you the process and helped you get better at it. Then, once you knew that process, you worked on improving and refining your skills . . . Before long, you developed the "know-how" for that activity—not just the skill to do it, but also an ability to be innovative and original . . . Writing is similar to the other things you enjoy doing. To write well, you first need to develop your own writing process. Strong writers aren't born with a specific gift and they aren't necessarily smarter than anyone else. Strong writers have simply learned and mastered a reliable writing process that allows them to generate new ideas and shape those ideas into something readers will find interesting and useful. (Johnson-Sheehan and Paine 2013, 8)

And Lunsford et al. (2016) note in the textbook *Everyone's an Author* that the writing process is highly individualized: "One important aspect of becoming comfortable with the writing process is figure out what works best for you. No single process works for every author or every writing task, so work instead to develop a repertoire of writing strategies that will enable you to become an efficient, productive, and effective writer." (79) Most composition textbooks offer similar descriptions of the writing process as an individualized and complex process to students. The interviews suggest that writing faculty preach what they experience as faculty writers.

Kathi Yancey notes in her threshold concept "Writers' Histories, Processes, and Identities Vary," composing processes vary according to at least three factors: (1) the individual writer, (2) the genre being composed, and (3) the rhetorical situation—and all three are especially relevant when describing our academic writing behaviors as writing faculty (Adler-Kassner and Wardle 2015, 52). It's no accident that interviewees offer the advice to start a writing project by thinking rhetorically because knowing the potential audience also means knowing where the final product might be published and what genre is required. Knowing their own individual proclivities as writers and adjusting for them helps writing faculty succeed in completing writing for publication (e.g., Jessica Enoch's awareness that she is a slow writer prompts her to write daily). Though interviewees share some of the same general attitudes and behaviors, each faculty writer writes from a different location, historical context, and understanding of the discipline, and these factors are always changing. As a result of these factors in flux, composing processes for academic publication naturally vary from interviewee to interviewee despite general attitudes and strategies they share. Moreover, the writing process is not a smooth singular process; interviews reveal that writing is intermittent, distributed over time, and may even be a series of smaller processes.

Because writing faculty experience writing as a process or series of processes, this experience affects how they approach everything from writer's block, to writing routines, to revision. This core disciplinary belief—that all writers write individually and writing is a complex, messy, and time-consuming process—illustrates a key difference between what writing faculty enact as academic writers and how university administrations and other disciplines view faculty writing. Higher education as an entity tends to conflate academic writing with publication where the publication, rather than the writing behind it, is emphasized. Because the academic writing process itself is invisible within academia, existing faculty development research treats it as either a task that can (and should) be hurried through using articles promising "Fast Article Writing Methodology" (Mikhailova and Nilson 2007) or as a minor stage in a larger (read: more important) research process where results are merely "written up" (i.e., suggested by faculty development titles such as Silva's 2015 *Write It Up* or Wollcott's 2009 *Writing Up Qualitative Research*). This culture of downplaying the academic writing process may also explain why academic writers in most disciplines don't refer to themselves as writers and prefer to call themselves researchers or scientists (Geller 2013; Toor 2015). As noted in the introduction, interviewees identify as writers. This disciplinary identity may explain why they engage in writing practices to reinforce that identity. Because these rhetoric and composition faculty believe writing is a process when they teach and when they research writing, our disciplinary location has a direct and positive impact on how we write. Further, interview research illustrates our published writing products are the fruition of writing processes that work.

Practicing writing as a process may help explain why these writing faculty succeed in publishing when research shows that many faculty fail. In a *Chronicle of Higher Education* article, Christopher Schaberg points out that though publishing is rewarding, "I'm not saying that writing is easy. It's hard. It's always a challenge to sit down and put in writing something that is coherent, clear, and persuasive. Life inevitably gets in the way. You try various methods—none of them seem to work, or not for long. Writing happens in spurts, or seems to resist you like a stubborn child" (Schaberg 2016, n.p.). Interviewees demonstrate that accepting writing as a challenging process, requiring thinking and frequent stops and starts, helps them work through this difficulty Schaberg describes. Though writing advice guides abound, the broad amount of research on faculty across disciplines who don't write (Boice and Jones 1984; Eagan and Garvey 2015; Fox 1992; Savage 2003) illustrates that having strategies for writing is not the only solution to making faculty more productive. This is not to say that concerns typically covered within faculty development scholarship such as time management, mentoring, responding to revise and resubmit letters appropriately, and the like are insignificant. In fact, when faced with a typical campus message that writing itself is undervalued in lieu of publication, research shows that many faculty in our discipline and others struggle to find a supportive writing environment and need help on many fronts, including practical writing matters. Yet short-term solutions promised by faculty development research may not help to develop sustainable academic writing behaviors that persist through changes in schedule, increasing faculty responsibilities, and unforeseen projects. "How to" resources are helpful (indeed, I use them myself, as do some of the interviewees here), but they don't always get to the underlying behaviors and attitudes that increase, sustain, and improve writing. Such texts tend to do the opposite because faculty development texts "tend to disregard that writing is a situated practice dependent on the activation of complex knowledge domains" (Scott 2014, 66). Writing faculty enact academic writing as a process, or series of processes, and our disciplinary position helps foster attitudes and writing techniques that work in combination for publication success.

WHERE DO WE GO FROM HERE? DIRECTIONS FOR FUTURE RESEARCH

Our disciplinary location clearly offers a strategic advantage to rethink how academic writing develops. The writing attitudes and strategies described in the introduction demonstrate a deep experience of writing as a process and are linked to their dual identities as writing teachers and scholars of rhetoric and composition. Moving forward, what do these conversations about faculty writing with rhetoric and composition offer in terms of research opportunities (i.e., unanswered questions) for our discipline?

First, because rhetoric and composition as a field is inextricably tied to pedagogy (Stenberg 2005), it is imperative that research on faculty writing must be done with an eye toward teaching. We identify as writers, we research writing, we write writing textbooks, and we teach writing. How do these subdisciplinary areas relate? What do our writing practices mean for our teaching practices? We might write with our students and occasionally share writing (see Harris and Tinberg), but how do our writing habits and feelings toward writing affect our professed pedagogical practices and vice versa? Though not the main focus of the interviews, it is clear that being a successful writer does offer some impact on teaching, both formally seen in interviews with Joe Harris, who offers his students the same questions he asks himself when he revises, and Cheryl Glenn, who models how she writes articles for her graduate students (both Glenn and Jessica Enoch, her former student in this collection, refer to this modeling as teaching).

Within the graduate classroom, the interview findings featured here might offer options for how to teach graduate students the writing practices of rhetoric and composition. Traditionally we might assign seminar papers or digital projects, yet Hayot (2014) notes that the end of semester seminar papers are unlikely to teach actual writing practices needed for academic publication due to the rushed nature of these assignments. Even if students are already strong writers, they don't necessarily understand the difference between writing and academic writing, because both types of writing have different goals (Elbow 1995; Gould, Katzmarek, and Shaw 2007). Detailed research is needed to see what we can transfer to graduate students from our own writing practices and what assignments might serve their interests as future authors better. Beyond seminar papers and writing for publication/digital publication courses in some doctoral programs, any additional graduate writing instruction within rhetoric and composition as a field has largely been the result of a one-to-one modeling (e.g., how Enoch learned from Glenn). We need to go beyond just modeling how we write for our graduate students and actually teach them how we know how to do it. Laura Micciche's work is a useful starting point here as she advocates for a deliberate space such as a class or workshop focused on teaching "critical" academic writing practice. Because much of writing for publication is engagement with previous scholarship, Micciche defines critical writing as the process of "building on others' ideas as well as challenging and recasting those ideas for different purposes and contexts" (Micciche and Carr 2011, 480). One of the patterns for analysis, thinking rhetorically, illustrates the interviewees are already doing this. Through deliberate instruction of this type we might encourage graduate students to envision academic writing differently.

Collaborative writing practices for publication offers another area for study, and this is an area where some research on co-authoring and rationales for choosing to write collaboratively within the field of writing studies exists (see Ede and Lunsford 1990, 2001; Roen et al. 1995; Ronald and Roskelly 2001; Yancey and Spooner 1998). Most of the interviewees have co-authored regularly, and rhetoric and composition has a long history of collaborative writing pairs (i.e., Andrea Lunsford and Lisa Ede, Duane Roen and Stuart Brown, and Gail Hawisher and Cynthia Selfe). Interview evidence also confirms earlier research (Ede and Lunsford 1990, 2001; Ronald and Roskelly 2001) noting many faculty writers in rhetoric and composition actively resist a traditional academic notion of carving out the work to individual authors. Selfe, for example, describes how she lets go of her writing when working with her longtime collaborator Gail Hawisher: "I'm not protective of my words. I want [writing collaborators] to actually mix it [the text] up with me in there. I don't want to be able to point to something and be like, "That's my paragraph" or "That's my idea." . . . Right now, honestly, if somebody asked me which parts of this work or that work were Gail's and which parts were mine . . . I wouldn't know." More exploration is needed to see if a preference for collaboration within the discipline affects collaborators as individual writers *after* the collaboration. In other words, does the collaborative process have any lasting influence on individual writers?

Research from these interviews indicates that writing faculty who collaborate establish how a collaboration will function prior to writing, which may be a first direction for this type of exploration. Kathi Yancey, for example, notes by asking pointed and specific questions about how a collaboration will function, collaborators lay out a map to finishing a writing task:

> How are you going to start? Is one of you going to draft one section, another of you is going to draft a different section, then you're going to swap? Or is somebody going to do basically a concept and then another person is going to take that concept and run with it and then swap it back and forth? When you swap back and forth are you going to use track changes [in Microsoft Word] or are you going to give people permission to overwrite your prose and you won't know where they changed it?

Kris Blair, Jessica Enoch, Thomas Rickert, Duane Roen, and Cindy Selfe all have clear methods for exchanging work that are useful and practical that illustrate how they answer Yancey's questions. The next step would be to look at how writing faculty may change as individual writers as a result of these collaborations. Interviews illustrate our collaboration patterns are complex, and we do have specific advice for making collaborations effective, making this a rich area for study.

Another place for future research is to look at how research into our own successful writing practice can help our institutions understand academic writing as both a product *and* a process. Writing is "the one constant across all academic disciplines" (Salem and Follett 2013, 57), and research on our own writing habits can enhance this discussion. These conversations offer a specificity that explains exactly how writing faculty are writing, particularly through the earliest process stages. The messiness and detail offered by these conversations directly contrasts with messages they may receive elsewhere in the institution where the emphasis is on publication, versus the writing needed to get to the publication. Salem and Follett note that this emphasis on publication only negatively affects faculty views of the academic writing process:

> eliminating the word "writing" from a discussion of faculty work also implies that the process one engages in to produce a published research manuscript is less meaningful than the fact of publication itself, eliding the hard work faculty *do* to achieve the publication. (Salem and Follett 2013, 57; emphasis added)

No faculty are more aware of this problem than writing faculty. Despite emphasizing a composing process with recursive stages of prewriting, drafting, and revision in writing courses, product is continually valued over process in the universities where we teach. And in our scholarly lives, product is valued as academic currency that enables us to develop robust scholarly reputations and move to more desirable faculty positions. These narrow ways of perceiving academic writing within faculty development and higher education in general downplay the complex thought and composing processes writing faculty describe in the interviews. While our experiences as writing faculty may not always transfer to faculty in other disciplines wholesale, nor should they, the interviews illustrate we know a lot about academic writing attitudes that help us manage frustration, habits such as writing in small bursts that are better suited to overscheduled faculty, and practices such as collaborative writing.

As noted in the introduction, one of the limitations of interviewing the rhetoric and composition "rock stars" was that most of these folks work at R1 institutions and that the interviews don't reveal as much about intersectionality and institutionality. Though the interviewees have heavy workloads due to teaching and administering writing, research shows that faculty at R1 institutions also have more perceived control over workload affecting attitudes toward a career as an academic (Perry et al. 2000). Therefore, another area for future exploration is to ask, How do local contexts such as community colleges and teaching institutions with 4–4 loads affect writing? The interview here by Howard Tinberg offers one look at how he writes as a rhetoric and composition faculty member at a community college (Townsend and Rosser [2009] does offer a look at community college faculty writers across disciplines), but there is little research about faculty working at small liberal arts colleges and regional universities. As noted in the author headnotes, many faculty such as Blair, Powell, and Yancey started at these non-flagship locations, and Royster previously worked at Spelman College, a historically black college. We need to know about writing lives at a variety of locations, because the interviewees' publication records illustrate they were able to publish enough at these early faculty positions to become mobile in the profession.

Another subset of writing faculty to research would be pre-tenure WPAs. Though traditional advice to new rhetoric and composition faculty is avoid directing a writing program until after tenure, many scholars push back on this idea, arguing that for some new faculty entering the field, WPA or WC work is the scholarship they conduct and waiting until year seven to start is unrealistic (Dew 2007). Research is needed to look at how new writing program directors are writing in these pre-tenure years to move beyond the implicit narrative that WPA work in the early years of one's career means less chance for publishing enough for tenure.

Beyond institutional context, looking at where race and gender affect writing within rhetoric and composition is essential. Research has shown faculty of color are disproportionately asked to serve on time consuming committees for diversity initiatives (Porter 2007; Rockquemore and Laszloffy 2008), which takes away valuable time from scholarship. There is also a clear negative correlation between research productivity and subtle race discrimination on campuses where faculty of color feel they have to work harder to prove themselves as scholars (Eagan and Garvey 2015; Griffin, Ward, and Phillips 2013). Women are disproportionately more likely to have publication slowdowns or stoppages due to birth of children or care for aging parents (Bianchi et al. 2012; Misra et al. 2011; Misra, Lundquist, and Templer 2012), and within rhetoric and composition, there are also accounts of fatherhood slowing productivity (Danberg 2011). Moreover, because a higher number of writing faculty are women (Ballif, Davis, and Mountford 2008; Skeffington, Borrowman, and Enos 2008), family care issues disproportionately affect those in rhetoric and composition positions, though scholars such as Marquez (2011) work to change these narratives. Beyond those challenges, in terms of sheer mathematics, all faculty are more likely to end up at comprehensive universities, liberal arts schools, and community colleges, yet have not been taught how to juggle publication expectations with heavy-teaching-load locations (Baldwin and Baker 2009; Mamiseishvili and Rosser 2011; Perry et al. 2000). More research is needed to understand how writing faculty write in these locations. While Howard Tinberg's interview offers a look at academic writing within the community college context, work is especially needed to look at community college writing faculty who publish as faculty responsibilities differ in these institutions, affecting publication (Townsend and Rosser 2009). The interviews certainly offer some helpful suggestions for starting and organizing writing projects as well as writing in short time segments, which may be useful for non-R1 types of institutions, but more research is needed into how institutions affect academic writing beyond studies of how more teaching or more service = less research.

Finally, we need to ask, What does "good" writing in the discipline actually look like? Chris Anson similarly refers to revision as a craft and makes the argument for valuing high quality academic writing as a field:

> I like writers who really craft their writing. I think too often we forget as compositionists, we want to be writing really well in addition to researching well. The field admits a really broad range of styles from almost clinical, empirical research, to more analytical stuff and interpretive stuff, such as case studies, to work I think of as being really highly crafted. The language itself becomes really important.

Anson is not alone. In her analysis of *Studies of Higher Education* articles, Helen Sword (2009) finds that though most academics claim to prefer reading academic articles that are well crafted, only six of the fifty articles she analyzed had well-crafted sentences. This is not surprising, as Savage (2003) describes in research on "forced productivity" in the university where faculty dutifully churn out publications without regard for the writing. Echoing the findings from the interviewees who work to develop well-crafted writing, Sword argues, "We owe it to our colleagues, our students, our institutions and, yes, to ourselves to write as the most effective teachers teach: with passion, with craft, with care and with style" (Sword 2009, 334). We enjoy well-crafted writing as a field, but there has yet to be research as to what we define as well-crafted writing within the field of rhetoric and composition. High quality academic writing within our field is unstudied, yet the interviews featured in *How Writing Faculty Write* suggest we know what it may look like. Many interviewees, for example, discussed stylish writers within the field and admired well-crafted disciplinary writing such as Doug Hesse's essayist writing style or Kathi Yancey's "theoretically infused, but so approachable" style (DeVoss, this collection). There is also a growing body of research on faculty academic writing structures and stylistic choices (Hayot 2014; Sandelowski 1998; Sword 2012) that primarily focuses on writing for literary disciplines, social sciences, or nursing. We like crafted writing in our own discipline as the interviewees suggest, and I'd like to see research on academic writing structures used effectively within rhetoric and composition publications, particularly because we teach structure in first-year writing but not necessarily style. The interviewees were quick to note who has a persuasive or engaging academic style and clearly paid attention to strong academic writing. In this case, the writing itself is just as important as the content and the resulting publication, but we haven't researched these issues of good academic writing in our discipline. Yet far from being a secondary concern to our teaching practices, or other areas more prominently featured in our research, Christina Crosby argues, "Our profession depends on the specialized writing we do for one another; success requires submitting one's writing to peer-reviewed journals and presses, with the goal of producing work that one's peers judge to merit publication" (Crosby 2003, 62–627). Most important, the interviews illustrate writing is an emotional process, along with a technical, physical, and mental process.

The time is opportune for rhetoric and composition to study faculty writing practices for publication within our discipline. The frank discussions featured here are a necessary first step to begin that research. Malea Powell points out in her interview, "We have to talk about our writing in some pretty honest ways for a long time before we start to develop a good vocabulary." As I wrote in the Preface, I was initially inspired by *The Paris Review* interviews because they capture writers talking about how they write, but these conversations started with someone asking good questions about writing. Encouraging writing faculty to talk more openly and explicitly about their writing processes offers rich terrain for studying what it means to be a professor who writes in the discipline.

AFTERWORD

It didn't seem right to write a book about faculty writing and argue we need more open discussion of our writing process while not revealing anything about my own writing process. The initial idea for *How Writing Faculty Write* stemmed from a 2009 National Public Radio story I read about the "Writers at Work" series from Maud Newton and her descriptions of the wealth of advice given by prolific authors (Newton 2009). After reading these interviews myself, I liked the structure and used this as the overarching idea for the project, as well as a model for questions I might ask writing faculty. After completing the interviews, because I had them recorded, I often played them in my car on the way to work and wrote down ideas for topics I wanted to raise in the introduction and conclusion on the back of my toddler's coloring book because it was usually thrown in the front seat. I ripped off that back cover and taped it to the wall above my desk at work and developed a Microsoft Word document that contained a list of what faculty kept saying over and over, and cut and pasted in quotes from the transcripts of who said what.

From there, I read everything on faculty writing and productivity I could get my hands on. Every two or three articles I stopped reading and pulled out quotes I knew I wanted to use by cutting and pasting them in the initial Microsoft Word document near the faculty interviews that they corresponded with. As I read more, I put "like" quotes and interview excerpts together and developed subheadings that grouped them in some way. Once I had about ten pages of quotes, I wrote a separate document of everything I wanted to say to introduce the collection and dropped in relevant support from the first document. Starting fresh, with my own voice, helped me put in more of my own writing. I paraphrased from sources more and cut down interview excerpts to just the essentials. To complete the above writing process, I worked in three specific ways. Two days a week I wrote for two hours a day using the timer on my phone and a new library location each time. I'd find a new corner, hit the timer on my phone, and write. The other three days I wrote in the small pockets interviewees describe. To prepare for these speed writing sessions, after completing a longer writing session the day before, I would print out a new draft. In the few minutes between classes and meetings during the next day (which often totaled between

DOI: 10.7330/9781607326625.c017

fourteen and twenty-two minutes), I reread sections and made small edits, found sentences that didn't make sense, and worked to fix these. I used this marked up paper draft to start the longer writing session the next day. After putting in the edits from the day before, because I had again familiarized myself with the draft I could begin writing again. And some days I just skipped writing to take a day off. With two small kids at home, I also rarely wrote on weekends.

In many ways, I do what the writing faculty featured here do. Interviewees note that having passion for a project before starting it helps move writing forward, and in my case, this was true. Even if I didn't feel like writing on a particular day (especially on the days when I wrote for just a few minutes at a time), only a few minutes in helped me get interested all over again. I also took advantage of two other strategies interviewees mentioned. One, I asked every faculty member I knew about his or her writing process (both in rhetoric and composition and outside of it). The more I talked to faculty about how they wrote, the easier it was for me to see connections in my book and think rhetorically about who might care about what I was saying. Two, I toggled between working on this book and other articles and projects. In my two-hour writing days, I might work on the book for a half hour, but then work on page proofs for another project closer to publication so I didn't burn out on the topic. Finally, I stuck a Post-it on my open laptop that listed reasons why someone would want to read this collection, to keep in mind both the main goal of the project but also information that helped me complete the initial book proposal.

APPENDIX
Interview Questions

The following represent the type of general questions I asked in faculty interviews. As noted in the methodology description, I also asked individual questions of each writer. I encourage readers to use these to explore writing at work.

How do you feel when you write?

Do you have any writing rituals or habits?

How do you start a writing project?

Is there a difference between composing for a digital publication versus a print publication?

Do you ever get writer's block?

What do you do when you can't write?

Do you offer students writing advice that you also follow?

What is your dream writing project that you haven't been able to write yet?

How do you revise your work?

How do you collaborate with others when writing?

Are there productivity strategies that work especially well for you?

How do you juggle multiple projects?

How have your writing habits changed from graduate school?

What does a typical writing day look like?

Is there a published piece you wish you could now go back and revise?

Do you see yourself as a rhetoric or composition scholar, or both, in your work?

Whose writing do you admire in the field?

DOI: 10.7330/9781607326625.c018

REFERENCES

Adler-Kassner, Linda, and Elizabeth Wardle. 2015. *aming What We Know: Threshold Concepts of Writing Studies.* Logan: Utah State University Press.

Alexander, Jonathan. 2015. "From the Editor." *College Composition and Communication* 66 (3): 380–83.

Alred, Gerald J., and Erik A. Thelen. 1993. "Are Textbooks Contributions to Scholarship?" *College Composition and Communication* 44 (4): 466–477. https://doi.org/10.2307/358382.

Applebee, Arthur N. 1977. *A Survey of Teaching Conditions in English.* Urbana: National Council of Teachers of English.

Attride-Stirling, Jennifer. 2001. "Thematic Networks: An Analytical Tool for Qualitative Research." *Qualitative Research* 1 (3): 385–405. https://doi.org/10.1177/146879410100100307.

Baldwin, Claire, and Genevieve Chandler. 2002. "Improving Faculty Publication Output: The Role of a Writing Coach." *Journal of Professional Nursing* 18 (1): 8–15. https://doi.org/10.1053/jpnu.2002.30896.

Baldwin, Roger, and Vicki Baker. 2009. "The Case of the Disappearing Liberal Arts College." *Inside Higher Ed* (July 9). https://www.insidehighered.com/views/2009/07/09/baldwin.

Ball, Cheryl E. 2004. "Show, Not Tell: The Value of New Media Scholarship." *Computers and Composition* 21 (4): 403–425. https://doi.org/10.1016/S8755-4615(04)00038-6.

Ballif, Michelle, D. Diane Davis, and Roxanne Mountford. 2008. *Women's Ways of Making It in Rhetoric and Composition.* New York: Routledge.

Belcher, Wendy Laura. 2009. *Writing Your Journal Article in 12 Weeks: A Guide to Academic Publishing Success.* Thousand Oaks: Sage.

Bellas, Marcia L., and Robert K. Toutkoushian. 1999. "Faculty Time Allocations and Research Productivity: Gender, Race, and Family Effects." *Review of Higher Education* 22 (4): 367–390. https://doi.org/10.1353/rhe.1999.0014.

Bernhardt, Stephen A., Penny Edwards, and Patti Wojahn. 1989. "Teaching College Composition with Computers: A Program Evaluation Study." *Written Communication* 6 (1): 108–133. https://doi.org/10.1177/0741088389006001007.

Bianchi, Suzanne M., Liana C. Sayer, Melissa A. Milkie, and John P. Robinson. 2012. "Housework: Who Did, Does or Will Do It, and How Much Does It Matter?" *Social Forces* 91 (1): 55–63. https://doi.org/10.1093/sf/sos120.

Boice, Robert. 1985. "The Neglected Third Factor in Writing: Productivity." *College Composition and Communication* 36 (4): 472–480. https://doi.org/10.2307/357866.

Boice, Robert. 1990. *Professors as Writers: A Self-Help Guide to Productive Writing.* Stillwater: New Forums Press.

Boice, Robert, and Ferdinand Jones. 1984. "Why Academicians Don't Write." *Journal of Higher Education* 55 (5): 567–582. https://doi.org/10.1080/00221546.1984.11780679.

Brannon, Lil, and Gordon Pradl. 1994. "The Socialization of Writing Teachers." *Journal of Basic Writing* 3 (4): 28–37.

Briggs, Charles. 2000. "Interview." *Journal of Linguistic Anthropology* 9 (1–2): 137–40.

Brooks, Van Wyck. 1963. "Introduction." *Writers at Work: The Paris Review Interviews.* Second Series. New York: Viking.

DOI: 10.7330/9781607326625.c019

Brooks-Gillies, Marilee, Elena G. Garcia, Soo Hyon Kim, Katie Manthey, and Trixie Smith. 2015. "Graduate Writing Across the Disciplines, Introduction." *Across the Disciplines 12.* https://wac.colostate.edu/atd/graduate_wac/intro.cfm.

Brown, Amy Benson. 2014. "Helen Sword on Empowerment and Academic Writing: Excerpts from an Interview." *Academic Coaching & Writing.* https://www.academiccoachingandwriting.org/academic-writing/academic-writing-blog/reference-list-formatting/reference-list-formatting/helen-sword-on-academic-writing.

Caplan, Nigel, and Michelle Cox. 2016. "The State of Graduate Communication Support: Results of an International Survey." In *Supporting Graduate Student Writers: Research, Support, and Curriculum Design,* ed. Steve Simpson, Nigel A. Caplan, Michelle Cox, and Talinn Phillips, 22–51. Ann Arbor: University of Michigan Press.

Carnell, Eileen, Jacqui MacDonald, Bet McCallum, and Mary Scott. 2008. *Passion and Politics: Academics Reflect on Writing for Publication.* London: University of London.

Conference on College Composition and Communication. 1982. "Position Statement on the Preparation and Professional Development of Teachers of Writing." http://cccc.ncte.org/cccc/resources/positions/statementonprep.

Connors, Robert J. 1990. "Overwork/Underpay: Labor and Status of Composition Teachers Since 1880." *Rhetoric Review* 9 (1): 108–126. https://doi.org/10.1080/07350199009388919.

Council of Writing Program Administrators. 2011. "Framework for Success in Postsecondary Writing." http://wpacouncil.org/files/framework-for-success-postsecondary-writing.pdf.

Cowley, Malcolm, ed. 1967 (1958). *Writers at Work: The Paris Review Interviews. Rpt.* New York: Viking Press.

Crosby, Christina. 2003. "Writer's Block, Merit, and the Market: Working in the University of Excellence." *College English* 65 (6): 626–645. https://doi.org/10.2307/3594274.

Crowley, Sharon. 2010. *The Methodical Memory: Invention in Current-Traditional Rhetoric.* Carbondale: Southern Illinois University Press.

Danberg, Robert. 2011. "On (Not) Making It in Rhetoric and Composition." *Composition Studies* 39 (1): 63–72.

Dangler, Doug. 2010. "Multimodal Composition and the Rhetoric of Teaching: A Conversation with Cheryl Ball." *Issues in Writing* 18 (1): 111–31.

Day, Kami, and Michele Eodice. 2001. *(First Person)^2: A Study of Co-Authoring in the Academy.* Logan: Utah State University Press.

Dew, Debra Frank. 2007. "Labor Relations: Collaring jWPA Desire." In *Untenured Faculty as Writing Program Administrators: Institutional Practices and Politics,* ed. Debra F. Dew and Alice S. Horning, 110–36. West Lafayette: Parlor Press.

Dwyer, Angela, Bridget Lewis, Fiona McDonald, and Marcelle Burns. 2012. "It's Always a Pleasure: Exploring Productivity and Pleasure in a Writing Group for Early Career Academics." *Studies in Continuing Education* 34 (2): 129–144. https://doi.org/10.1080/0158037X.2011.580734.

Eagan, M. Kevin, Jr., and Jason C. Garvey. 2015. "Stressing Out: Connecting Race, Gender, and Stress with Faculty Productivity." *Journal of Higher Education* 86 (6): 923–954. https://doi.org/10.1080/00221546.2015.11777389.

Ede, Lisa, and Andrea A. Lunsford. 2001. "Collaboration and Concepts of Authorship." *PMLA* 116 (2): 354–69.

Ede, Lisa, and Andrea Lunsford. 1990. *Singular Texts/Plural Authors: Perspectives on Collaborative Writing.* Carbondale: Southern Illinois University Press.

Elbow, Peter. 1987. "Closing My Eyes as I Speak: An Argument for Ignoring Audience." *College English* 49 (1): 50–69. https://doi.org/10.2307/377789.

Elbow, Peter. 1995. "Being a Writer vs. Being an Academic: A Conflict in Goals." *College Composition and Communication* 46 (1): 72–83. https://doi.org/10.2307/358871.

Elbow, Peter, and Mary Deane Sorcinelli. 2006. "The Faculty Writing Place: A Room of Our Own." *Change Magazine* (November/December): 17–22. https://doi.org/10.3200/CHNG.38.6.17-22.

Eodice, Michele, and Sharon Cramer. 2001. "Write On! A Model for Enhancing Faculty Publication." *Journal of Faculty Development* 18 (4): 113–21.

Eodice, Michele, and Anne Geller, eds. 2013. *Working with Faculty Writers*. Logan: Utah State University Press.

Eng, Joseph. 2002. "Teachers as Writers and Students as Writers: Writing, Publishing, and Monday-Morning Agendas." *Writing Instructor* 2 (5): n.p. http://writinginstructor.org.

Enos, Theresa. 1990. "Gender and Publishing." *Pre-Text: A Journal of Rhetorical Theory* 11 (3–4): 311–16.

Enos, Theresa. 1996. *Gender Roles and Faculty Lives in Rhetoric and Composition*. Carbondale: Southern Illinois University Press.

Enos, Theresa, Shane Borrowman, and Jillian Skeffington. 2008. *The Promise and Perils of Writing Program Administration*. West Lafayette: Parlor Press.

Fairweather, James S. 1999. "The Highly Productive Faculty Member: Confronting the Mythologies of Faculty Work." In *Faculty Productivity: Facts, Fictions, and Issues*, ed. William G. Tierney, 55–98. New York: Falmer Press.

Fairweather, James S. 2002. "The Mythologies of Faculty Productivity: Implications for Institutional Policy and Decision Making." *Journal of Higher Education* 73 (1): 26–48.

Fox, Mary F. 1992. "Research, Teaching, and Publication Productivity: Mutuality Versus Competition in Academia." *Sociology of Education* 65 (4): 293–305. https://doi.org/10.2307/2112772.

Gebhardt, Richard C. 1977. "Balancing Theory with Practice in the Training of Writing Teachers." *College Composition and Communication* 28 (2): 134–140. https://doi.org/10.2307/356098.

Gebhardt, Richard C., and Barbara Genelle Smith Gebhardt, eds. 1997. *Academic Advancement in Composition Studies: Scholarship, Publication, Promotion, Tenure*. Mahwah: Lawrence Erlbaum Associates.

Geller, Anne Ellen. 2013. "Introduction." In *Working with Faculty Writers*, ed. Anne E. Geller and Michele Eodice, 1–20. Logan: Utah State University Press.

Geller, Anne Ellen, and Harry Denny. 2013. "Of Ladybugs, Low Status, and Loving the Job: Writing Center Professionals Navigating Their Careers." *Writing Center Journal* 33 (1): 96–129.

Gindlesparger, Kathryn Johnson. 2011. "Snapshot of a Tenure Decision." *WPA. Writing Program Administration* 35 (1): 152–55.

Goggin, Maureen Daly. 2000. *Authoring a Discipline: Scholarly Journals and the Post–World War II Emergence of Rhetoric and Composition*. Mahwah: Lawrence Erlbaum.

Goodsen, Patricia. 2012. *Becoming an Academic Writer: 50 Exercises for Paced, Productive, and Powerful Writing*. Thousand Oaks: Sage.

Gould, J. Christine, JoAnne M. Katzmarek, and Patricia A. Shaw. 2007. "New Domains: Navigating the World of Academic Writing." *Phi Delta Kappan* 88 (10): 776–780. https://doi.org/10.1177/003172170708801017.

Grego, Rhonda C., and Nancy Thompson. 2007. *Teaching/Writing in Thirdspaces: The Studio Approach*. Carbondale: Southern Illinois University Press.

Griffin, Rachel Alicia, LaCharles Ward, and Amanda R. Phillips. 2013. "Still Flies in Buttermilk: Black Male Faculty, Critical Race Theory, and Composite Counterstorytelling." *International Journal of Qualitative Studies in Education: QSE* 27 (10): 1354–1375. https://doi.org/10.1080/09518398.2013.840403.

Hairston, Maxine. 1986. "When Writing Teachers Don't Write: Speculations about Probable Causes and Possible Cures." *Rhetoric Review* 5 (1): 62–70. https://doi.org/10.1080/07350198609359136.

Hardré, Patricia L. 2013. "The Power and Strategic Art of Revise-and-Resubmit: Maintaining Balance in Academic Publishing." *Journal of Faculty Development* 27 (1): 13–19.

Hardré, Patricia L., Andrea Beesley, Raymond Miller, and Terry Pace. 2011. "Faculty Motivation to do Research: Across Disciplines in Research-Extensive Universities." *Journal of the Professoriate* 5 (1): 35–69.

Hardré, Patricia L., and Sherry L. Kollmann. 2012. "Motivational Implications of Faculty Performance Standards." *Educational Management Administration & Leadership* 40 (6): 724–751. https://doi.org/10.1177/1741143212456913.

Haswell, Janis, and Richard Haswell. 2010. *Authoring: An Essay for the English Profession on Potentiality and Singularity*. Logan: Utah State University Press.

Hayot, Eric. 2014. *Elements of Academic Style: Writing for the Humanities*. New York: Columbia University Press. https://doi.org/10.7312/hayo16800.

Henderson, Bruce B. 2011. "Publishing Patterns at State Comprehensive Universities: The Changing Nature of Faculty Work and the Quest for Status." *Journal of the Professoriate* 5 (2): 35–66.

Howard, Jennifer. 2015. "College Jobs, Never Easy, Have Become Pressure Cookers." *The Chronicle of Higher Education* (July 9): n.p. http://chronicle.com/article/College-Jobs-Never-Easy-/231627/.

Jenkins, Rob. 2014. "Writing with a Heavy Teaching Load." *The Chronicle of Higher Education* (Jan 12): n.p. http://chronicle.com/article/Writing-With-a-Heavy-Teaching/151155/.

Johnson-Sheehan, Richard, and Charles Paine. 2013. *Writing Today*. 2nd ed. London: Pearson.

Kasper, Joseph. 2013. "An Academic with Imposter Syndrome." *The Chronicle of Higher Education* (April 3): n.p.: http://chronicle.com/article/An-Academic-With-Impostor/138231/.

Lechuga, Vicente M., and Deborah C. Lechuga. 2012. "Faculty Motivation and Scholarly Work: Self-Determination and Self-Regulation Perspectives." *Journal of the Professoriate* 6 (2): 59–97.

Leverenz, Carrie. 2000. "Tenure and Promotion in Rhetoric and Composition." *College Composition and Communication* 52 (1): 143–147. https://doi.org/10.2307/358549.

Lincoln, Yvonna S. 2011. "'A Well-Regulated Faculty . . .': The Coerciveness of Accountability and Other Measures That Abridge Faculties' Right to Teach and Research." *Cultural Studies, Critical Methodologies* 11 (4): 369–372. https://doi.org/10.1177/1532708611414668.

Look, Hugh, and Frances Pinter. 2010. "Open Access and Humanities and Social Science Monograph Publishing." *New Review of Academic Librarianship* 16 (S1): 90–97. https://doi.org/10.1080/13614533.2010.512244.

Lunsford, Andrea, Michal Brody, Lisa Ede, Beverly J. Moss, Carole Clark Papper, and Keith Walters. 2016. *Everyone's an Author with Readings*. 2nd ed. New York: W. W. Norton & Co.

Mamiseishvili, Ketevan, and Vicki J. Rosser. 2011. "Examining the Relationship between Faculty Productivity and Job Satisfaction." *Journal of the Professoriate* 5 (2): 100–132.

Marquez, Loren. 2011. "Narrating Our Lives: Retelling Mothering and Professional Work in Composition Studies." *Composition Studies* 39 (1): 73–85.

Mayrath, Michael C. 2008. "Attributions of Productive Authors in Educational Psychology Journals." *Educational Psychology Review* 20 (1): 41–56. https://doi.org/10.1007/s10648-007-9059-y.

McCormick, Ted. 2017. "Publish and Perish." *Chronicle of Higher Education* 63 (19). https://www.chronicle.com/article/PublishPerish/238816.

Micciche, Laura, and Allison D. Carr. 2011. "Toward Graduate Level Writing Instruction." *College Composition and Communication* 62 (3): 477–501.

Mikhailova, Elena A., and Linda B. Nilson. 2007. "Developing Prolific Scholars: The 'Fast Article Writing' Methodology." *Journal of Faculty Development* 21 (2): 93–100.

Minichiello, Victor, Rosalie Aroni, Eric Timewell, and Loris Alexander. 1990. *In-Depth Interviewing: Researching People.* Hong Kong: Longman Cheshire Pty Limited.

Misra, Joya, Jennifer Hickes Lundquist, Elissa Holmes, and Stephanie Agiomavritis. 2011. "The Ivory Ceiling of Service Work." *Academe* 97 (1): 22–26.

Misra, Joya, Jennifer Hickes Lundquist, and Abby Templer. 2012. "Gender, Work Time, and Care Responsibilities among Faculty." *Sociological Forum* 27 (2): 300–323. https://doi.org/10.1111/j.1573-7861.2012.01319.x.

Murray, Donald. 1984. *Write to Learn.* New York: Holt, Rinehart, and Winston.

Murray, Donald. 1986. "One Writer's Secrets." *College Composition and Communication* 37 (2): 146–153. https://doi.org/10.2307/357513.

Naylor, Charlie, and John Malcomson. 2001. "I Love Teaching English, but...": A Study of the Workload of English Teachers in B.C. in Secondary Grades." *British Columbia Teacher's Federation Report.* Section III. https://bctf.ca/publications/ResearchReports.aspx?id=5568.

Newton, Maud. 2009 (November 11). "Paris Review Author Interviews: 50 Years of Insight." *National Public Radio.* http://www.npr.org/templates/story/story.php?storyId=120303550.

Olson, Gary A., and Todd W. Taylor. 1997. *Publishing in Rhetoric and Composition.* Albany: State University of New York Press.

Ostman, Heather. 2013. *Writing Program Administration and the Community College.* Anderson: Parlor Press.

Packer, Colleen. 2013. "Educating Faculty for Gross Personal Happiness as Writers: An Analysis of Attitudes from a Faculty Writing Initiative." *Journal of the International Society for Teacher Education* 17 (1): 85–93.

Perry, Raymond P., Rodney Clifton, Verena H. Menec, Ward C. Struthers, and Robert J. Menges. 2000. "Faculty in Transition: A Longitudinal Analysis of Perceived Control and Type of Institution in the Research Productivity of Newly Hired Faculty." *Research in Higher Education* 41 (2): 165–194. https://doi.org/10.1023/A:1007091104399.

Phelps, Louise Wetherbee. 1998. *Composition as a Human Science: Contributions to the Self-Understanding of a Discipline.* Oxford: Oxford University Press.

Porter, Stephen R. 2007. "A Closer Look at Faculty Service: What Affects Participation on Committees?" *Journal of Higher Education* 78 (5): 523–541. https://doi.org/10.1080/00221546.2007.11772328.

Reid, E. Shelley. 2009. "Teaching Writing Teachers Writing: Difficulty, Exploration, and Critical Reflection." *College Composition and Communication* 61 (2): W197–W221.

Reinheimer, David A. 2005. "Teaching Composition Online: Whose Side Is Time On?" *Computers and Composition* 22 (4): 459–470. https://doi.org/10.1016/j.compcom.2005.08.004.

Rockquemore, Kerry, and Tracey A. Laszloffy. 2008. *The Black Academic's Guide to Winning Tenure—Without Losing Your Soul.* Boulder: Lynne Rienner Publishers.

Roen, Duane H., Victor Villanueva, Stuart Brown, Gesa Kirsch, John Adams, Susan Wyche-Smith, and Sheri Helsley. 1995. "Revising for Publication: Advice to Graduate Students and Other Junior Scholars." *Rhetoric Society Quarterly* 25 (1–4): 237–246. https://doi.org/10.1080/02773949509391047.

Ronald, Kate, and Hephzibiah Roskelly. 2001. "Learning to Take It Personally." In *Personal Effects: The Social Character of Scholarly Writing,* ed. Deborah H. Holdstein and David Bleich, 253–366. Logan: Utah State University Press.

Rose, Mike, and Karen A. McClafferty. 2001. "A Call for the Teaching of Writing in Graduate Education." *Educational Researcher* 30 (2): 27–33. https://doi.org/10.3102/0013189X030002027.

Russell, David R. 2002. *Writing in the Academic Disciplines: A Curricular History.* 2nd ed. Carbondale: Southern Illinois Press.

Salem, Lori, and Jennifer Follett. 2013. "The Idea of a Faculty Writing Center: Moving from Troubling Deficiencies to Collaborative Engagement." *Working with Faculty Writers*, ed. Anne Ellen Geller and Michele Eodice, 50–72. Logan: Utah State University Press.

Sallee, Margaret, Ronald Hallett, and William Tierney. 2011. "Teaching Writing in Graduate School." *College Teaching* 59 (2): 66–72. https://doi.org/10.1080/87567555.2010.511315.

Sandelowski, Margarete. 1998. "Writing a Good Read: Strategies for Re-presenting Qualitative Data." *Research in Nursing & Health* 21 (4): 375–382. https://doi.org/10.1002/(SICI)1098-240X(199808)21:4<375::AID-NUR9>3.0.CO;2-C.

Savage Jr., William W. 2003. "Scribble, Scribble Toil and Trouble: Forced Productivity in the Modern University." *Journal of Scholarly Publishing* 35 (1): 40–46.

Schaberg, Christopher. 2016. "Publish and Perish? Yes. Embrace It." The Chronicle of Higher Education (February 16): n.p. http://www.chronicle.com/article/Publish-or-Perish-Yes/235319?cid=rclink.

Scott, Andrea. 2014. "On Writer's Block: A Study of Disciplinary Negotiations in the Faculty Office and Classroom." *CEA Forum* 43 (1): 62–81.

Scott, Greg M., and Roberta Garner. 2013. *Doing Qualitative Research: Designs, Methods, and Techniques.* Boston: Pearson.

Semenza, Gregory. 2014. "The Value of Ten Minutes: Writing Advice for the Time-Less Academic." *The Chronicle of Higher Education* (July 18): n.p. https://chroniclevitae.com/news/616-the-value-of-10-minutes-writing-advice-for-the-time-less-academic.

Shahjahan, Riyad. 2014. *Developing the Resilient Writing Spirit: How to Overcome Shame and Impostor Feelings.* Presentation for the National Center for Faculty Development and Diversity. Online; Accessed October 20, 2014.

Skeffington, Jillian, Shane Borrowman, and Theresa Enos. 2008. "Living in the Spaces Between: Profiling the Writing Program Administrator." In *The Promise and Perils of Writing Program Administration*, ed. Theresa Enos and Shane Borrowman, 5–20. West Lafayette: Parlor Press.

Smith, Matt. 2008. "Writing Program Administration and the Small University." In *The Promise and Perils of Writing Program Administration*, ed. Theresa Enos and Shane Borrowman, 117–25. West Lafayette: Parlor Press.

Soderlund, Lars. 2015. "Findings: Identifying and Sharing Habits for Productive Practices." Paper presented at the annual meeting for the *Conference on College Composition and Communication*, Tampa Bay, Florida, March 20.

Steinert, Yvonne, Peter J. McLeod, Stephen Liben, and Linda Snell. 2008. "Writing for Publication in Medical Education: The Benefits of a Faculty Development Workshop and Peer Writing Group." *Medical Teacher* 30 (8): 280–85. https://doi.org/10.1080/01421590802337120.

Stenberg, Shari. 2005. *Professing and Pedagogy: Learning the Teaching of English.* Urbana: NCTE.

Stupnisky, Robert, Marcus Weaver-Hightower, and Yulyia Kartoshkina. 2015. "Exploring and Testing the Predictors of New Faculty Success: A Mixed Methods Study." *Studies in Higher Education* 40 (2): 368–390. https://doi.org/10.1080/03075079.2013.842220.

Sword, Helen. 2009. "Writing Higher Education Differently: A Manifesto on Style." *Studies in Higher Education* 34 (3): 319–336. https://doi.org/10.1080/03075070802597101.

Sword, Helen. 2012. *Stylish Academic Writing.* Cambridge: Harvard University Press.

Takayoshi, Pamela, and Cynthia L. Selfe. 2007. "Thinking about Multimodality." In *Multimodal Composition: Resources for Teachers*, ed. Cynthia L. Selfe, 1–12. Cresskill: Hampton Press.

Thaiss, Christopher, and Terry Myers Zawacki. 2006. *Engaged Writers and Dynamic Disciplines: Research on the Academic Writing Life.* Portsmouth: Boynton/Cook.

Thrower, Peter. 2012. "Eight Reasons I Rejected Your Article." *Elsevier Connect*. https://www.elsevier.com/connect/8-reasons-i-rejected-your-article.

Tien, Flora F., and Robert T. Blackburn. 1996. "Faculty Rank System, Research Motivation, and Faculty Research Productivity: Measure Refinement and Theory Testing." *Journal of Higher Education* 67 (1): 2–22. https://doi.org/10.1080/00221546.1996.11780246.

Toor, Rachel. 2015. "Scholars Talk Writing: Anthony Grafton." http://racheltoor.com/scholars-talk-writing-anthony-grafton/. *Chronicle of Higher Education*, September 12.

Townsend, Barbara K., and Vicki J. Rosser. 2007. "Workload Issues and Measures of Faculty Productivity." *Thought & Action* 23:7–20.

Townsend, Barbara K., and Vicki J. Rosser. 2009. "The Extent and Nature of Scholarly Activities among Community College Faculty." *Community College Journal of Research and Practice* 33 (9): 669–81. https://doi.org/10.1080/10668920902921502.

Trice, Andrea, J. 1992. "The Tensions between Teaching and Scholarship." *Chronicle of Higher Education* (June 17): B4.

Tulley, Christine. 2008. "Negotiating Digital and Traditional Literacies: Training Non-Traditional Preservice Writing Teachers." *Computers and Composition Online*. Accessed March 14, 2014. http://www2.bgsu.edu/departments/english/cconline/Negotiating/default.html.

Tulley, Christine. 2013. *How to Develop a Faculty Writing Group at a Teaching-Intensive University*. Presentation for the National Center for Faculty Development and Diversity. Online; Accessed March 26, 2013.

Wardle, Elizabeth, and Doug Downs. 2017. *Writing about Writing: A College Reader*. 3rd ed. Boston: Bedford/St. Martin's.

Webber, Karen L. 2011. "Factors Related to Faculty Research Productivity and Implications for Academic Planners." *Planning for Higher Education* 39 (4): 32–43.

Wells, Jaclyn. 2015. "Methods: Investigating the Research and Writing Practices of Rhetoric and Composition Scholars." Paper presented at the annual meeting for the *Conference on College Composition and Communication*, Tampa Bay, Florida, March 20.

Wilson, Robin. 2010. "The Ivory Sweatshop: Academe Is No Longer a Convivial Refuge." *Chronicle of Higher Education* 56:B28–B32.

Yancey, Kathleen B., and Michael Spooner. 1998. "A Single Good Mind: Collaboration, Cooperation, and the Writing Self." *College Composition and Communication* 49 (1): 45–62. https://doi.org/10.2307/358559.

Zhang, Yan, and Barbara M. Wildemuth, 2009. "Unstructured Interviews." In *Applications of Social Research Methods to Questions in Information and Library Science*, ed. Barbara Wildemuth, 222–31. Westport: Libraries Unlimited.

ABOUT THE AUTHOR

Christine E. Tulley is professor of rhetoric and writing and founder and director of the Master of Arts in Rhetoric and Writing Program at the University of Findlay. She also serves as the Academic Career Development Coordinator for the UF Center for Teaching Excellence to support faculty scholarship productivity on campus. She is the former Praxis section editor for *Kairos: A Journal of Rhetoric, Technology, and Pedagogy*, the reviews editor for *Computers and Composition*, and winner of the Ellen Nold Award for Best Article in Computers and Composition for 2014.

INDEX